THIS JOURNAL BELONGS TO:

_____

If Found, Please Contact

ADDRESS: _____

_____

_____

PHONE: _____

EMAIL: _____

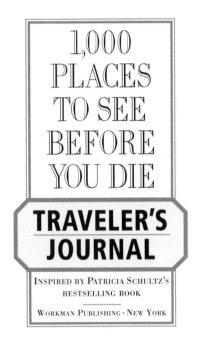

1,000 PLACES TO SEE BEFORE YOU DIE

TRAVELER'S JOURNAL

INSPIRED BY PATRICIA SCHULTZ'S
BESTSELLING BOOK

WORKMAN PUBLISHING · NEW YORK

A 1,000... BEFORE YOU DIE™ BOOK

PLACE: .... DATE: ....

PLACE: .... DATE: ....

"There are only two ways to live your life. One is as though nothing is a miracle. The other is as if everything is." —ALBERT EINSTEIN

PLACE: .... DATE: ....

PLACE: .... DATE: ....

PLACE: .... DATE: ....

PLACE: .... DATE: ....

"Throw your dreams into space like a kite, and you do not know what it will bring back, a new life, a new friend, a new love, a new country." —ANAÏS NIN

PLACE:... DATE:.................................

PLACE: .... DATE: ....

PLACE:.. DATE:......................

"**T**ake the Adventure, heed the call, now ere the irrevocable moment passes!" —KENNETH GRAHAME

PLACE: .... DATE: ....

Ten Experiences Guaranteed to Give You the Shivers

1. Witnessing the daily migration of bats from Carlsbad Caverns, New Mexico. In summer hundreds of thousands of Mexican free-tailed bats stream out of the caves, filling the sky for miles.

2. Viewing the life-size terra-cotta warriors of Xi'an, China. The Emperor Ch'in Shih Huang-ti commissioned this army of 7,000 soldiers (each one different from the others) in the 3rd century B.C. to guard his tomb.

3. Diving among the ghost fleet submerged in Chuuk Lagoon, Micronesia. On February 17, 1944, the U.S. military bombed Japanese warships in a surprise attack. Swimming among the 60 ruins, alive with brilliant marine life, is eerily gorgeous.

4. Roaming Vlad the Impaler's medieval castle in Transylvania, Romania. Although Prince Vlad Dracula of Walachia was never known to drink blood, his cruelty (impaling enemies alive on enormous stakes) inspired Bram Stoker's character Count Dracula.

5. Exploring the otherworldly landscape of the Badlands, South Dakota. 500,000 years of erosion have carved an alien landscape that General Alfred Sully described as "hell with the fires burned out."

6. Venturing on a nighttime safari in Kenya. Experience the bush that never sleeps. When your Masai guide shines his spotlight into the curtain of darkness, a sea of eyeballs lights up. Who is watching whom?

7. Sailing through the ice floes of Antarctica. Listen to the deafening silence in this limitless landscape of ice, sea, and sky, with its total absence of human presence.

8. Watching streams of Buddhist monks emerge at sunrise in Ladakh, India. Their robes all shades of crimson and saffron, the monks set off at the day's first light with their alms bowls to collect food and offerings.

Nature's chilling theatricality on display at the Badlands

9. Indulging in dinner at Taillevent in Paris, France. This gastronomic temple treats you like royalty, has clairvoyant service that sparkles and a wine cellar of more than 25,000 bottles, and the food is fit for the gods.

10. Bundling up at The Ice Hotel in Sweden. Snuggle between the reindeer pelts heaped on your ice bed in the only hotel in Europe constructed entirely of densely packed snow and ice—4,000 tons of it!

PLACE: .... DATE: ....

PLACE: .... DATE: ....

PLACE: .... DATE: ....

PLACE: .... DATE: ....

"To reach a port we must sail, sometimes with the wind and sometimes against it. But we must not drift or lie at anchor."
—OLIVER WENDELL HOLMES

PLACE: .... DATE: ....

PLACE: .... DATE: ....

PLACE: .... DATE: ....

"Life is not measured by the number of breaths we take but by the places and moments that take our breath away." —ANONYMOUS

PLACE: .... DATE: ....

PLACE: .... DATE: ....

PLACE: .... DATE: ....

PLACE: .... DATE: ....

"Those who wander are not necessarily lost." —J. R. R. TOLKIEN

PLACE: .... DATE: ....

PLACE: .... DATE: ....

PLACE: .... DATE: ....

"The longer I live, the more my mind dwells upon the beauty and wonder of the world." —JOHN BURROUGHS

PLACE: .... DATE: ....

Six Ephemeral Masterworks of Nature

1. Cherry blossoms, Yoshino Mountain, Japan. Every April, after the bleak winter skies clear, gentle spring breezes carry pink and white petals that flutter to the ground like snowflakes. Connoisseurs head for Yoshino Mountain, which is covered in thousands of white mountain cherry trees dating back to the days of the samurai—and whose delicate blossoms last only a couple of weeks.

Petals and people carpet the ground at Yoshino.

2. Lunar rainbows, Victoria Falls, Zimbabwe. The falls are every bit as monumental and magnificent as you imagined—a mile wide, crashing down 400 feet, making a noise greater than a million migrating wildebeests. But the mist creates more delicate visuals—rainbows in the day, and at night, if the moon is bright and full enough, lunar rainbows that drift in and out of view.

3. The coral spawn at Heron Island, Australia. Unlike many islands of the Great Barrier Reef, Heron is a coral cay—actually part of the reef itself. Each November, when the coral spawns, the polyps disgorge billions of pink and purple eggs and sperm. For divers, who come from every corner of the globe, it's like being inside of a rosy snowstorm.

4. Disappearing glaciers, Glacier National Park, Montana. The glaciers that formed this northernmost part of the American Rockies, carving out the awe-inspiring landscape, have done their work over the past several millennia. But their days are numbered. A little more than a century ago there were 150 named glaciers in the park; today there are only 37. At this rate, the glaciers will all but disappear by 2030. Visit the park soon while you can still marvel at these vanishing beauties.

5. Monarch butterfly migration, Michoacán, Mexico. Every autumn, like clockwork, millions of orange-and-black-winged monarch butterflies migrate from the eastern United States and Canada and arrive, as if from out of nowhere, to alight on the green fir trees northwest of Mexico City. They are so numerous that when they fly, the sky appears filled with orange and yellow confetti and you can hear their wings beating—and the combined weight of their tiny bodies can actually break the limbs off the trees.

6. The Northern Lights, Manitoba, Canada. During clear winter nights, arctic winds collide with the electron-charged atmosphere of the earth, creating eerily massive and silent aurora borealis, shimmering across the sky in spectacular colors.

PLACE: .... DATE: ....

PLACE: .... DATE: ....

PLACE: .... DATE: ....

"Live in the sunshine, swim the sea, drink the wild air's salubrity."
—RALPH WALDO EMERSON

PLACE: .... DATE: ....

PLACE: .... DATE: ....

PLACE: .... DATE: ....

PLACE: .... DATE: ....

"Abroad is the place where we stay up late, follow impulse and find ourselves as wide open as when we are in love." —PICO IYER

PLACE: .... DATE: ....

PLACE: .... DATE: ....

PLACE: .... DATE: ....

PLACE: .... DATE: ....

"The trail is the thing, not the end of the trail. Travel too fast and you miss all you are traveling for." —LOUIS L'AMOUR

PLACE: .... DATE: ....

PLACE: .... DATE: ....

EIGHT THINGS TO HEAR BEFORE YOU DIE

1. The call to prayer, Old Cairo, Egypt. Old Cairo is a symphony—no, a cacophony—of belching buses, chattering voices, and street vendors hawking their

The minarets of Cairo

wares. But just as the spires of Cairo's countless minarets puncture the dusty skyline, the muezzins' calls to prayer, five times each day, pierce the earthly din with their cries that lift to heaven.

2. The Santa Fe Opera, Santa Fe, New Mexico. Founded in 1957, the Santa Fe Opera has earned a reputation for innovative programs. Its glorious setting, an indoor/outdoor amphitheater carved into a hillside at the foot of the Sangre de Christo Mountains, clearly inspires a company that is revered for showcasing well-known international talents as well as discovering tomorrow's great voices.

3. Gregorian chant at San Miniato, Florence, Italy. Florence's oldest church, an 11th-century Romanesque structure with panoramic views from its perch on the city's highest hill, is a meditative setting. Every afternoon at dusk, Gregorian chants—those simple, timeless harmonics—will transport you back to the Middle Ages.

4. The absolute silence of Doubtful Sound, New Zealand. Only two boats operate in Doubtful Sound, one of the world's most magical and remote places. When your captain cuts the engine, you are surrounded by nature that's primeval in its beauty and that's enveloped in a silence that feels millennia-old.

5. The roar of the crowd, Fenway Park, Boston. Fenway is one of baseball's dowdy, uncomfortable old parks, but the Red Sox are baseball's comeback kids—and the hometown fans are the loudest, most impassioned bunch in the world. Leave your Yankees cap at home and revel in the heartfelt pandemonium of it all.

6. Early morning birdsong, Asa Wright Nature Center, Arima, Trinidad. Waking to the song of the more than 460 species of birds that live in the rain forest surrounding this former plantation is like waking to your own personal philharmonic—an exhilarating way to greet the day.

7. The snapping of prayer flags at the Boudhanath Stupa, Kathmandu, Nepal. The Buddhist monks who live at Boudhanath begin their day with morning *pujas* at 5:30, but even when their chanting has ended, the thin mountain air is always alive with the sound of the prayer flags snapping.

8. The Ryman Auditorium, Nashville, Tennessee. It's no wonder they call Nashville "Music City"—you can hear an undiscovered talent on any corner. But the best acoustics are at the Ryman, known as "the Mother Church of Country Music," and when a hometown favorite like Lucinda Williams takes the stage, you'll think you've died and gone to heaven.

PLACE: .... DATE: ....

PLACE: .... DATE: ....

"To awaken in a strange town is one of the most pleasant sensations
in the world." —FREYA STARK

PLACE: .... DATE: ....

PLACE: .... DATE: ....

PLACE: .... DATE: ....

"I travel for travel's sake. The great affair is to move; to feel the needs and hitches of our life more nearly; to come down off this feather-bed of civilization, and find the globe granite underfoot and strewn with cutting flints." —ROBERT LOUIS STEVENSON

PLACE: .... DATE: ....

PLACE: .... DATE: ....

PLACE: .... DATE: ....

PLACE: .... DATE: ....

"The real voyage of discovery consists not in seeking new landscapes but in having new eyes." —MARCEL PROUST

PLACE: .... DATE: ....

PLACE: .... DATE: ....

PLACE: .... DATE: ....

PLACE: .... DATE: ....

PLACE: .... DATE: ....

"Have we not stood here like trees in the ground long enough?"
—WALT WHITMAN

PLACE: .... DATE: ....

SEVEN PLACES WHERE TIME SEEMS TO STAND STILL

1. Raffles Hotel, Singapore. After an extensive renovation, one of Asia's great colonial landmarks emerged from its face-lift with its soul still intact. The Writers Bar (watering hole for Rudyard Kipling and Joseph Conrad) takes you right back to the days when Somerset Maugham bellied up for his favorite Million Dollar Cocktail.

2. The Island of Lamu, Kenya. A mix of ancient Swahili and Islamic cultures, the port of Lamu is Kenya's oldest living city. Donkeys roam its narrow streets; the men wear white robes and caps; the women, black purdah. Graceful dhows still ply the waters off the coast, and you can easily find one that will take you for a sunset sail.

3. Pompeii, Italy. Like the Pyramids, Pompeii is familiar to any school child, but nothing prepares you for a visit to the world's most famous ruins, where an entire once-flourishing town was buried (and preserved) under 20 feet of volcanic ash in A.D. 69 when the nearby volcano Mt. Vesuvius erupted with little notice. It's as if the ancient Romans had left only yesterday.

4. Amish Country, Shipshewana, Indiana. Horse-and-buggies start arriving at dawn for the weekly auction where farmers in wide-brimmed hats and Old Testament beards bid on hand-powered tools, kitchenware—even old wringer washing machines. Friday's horse and pony auction shouldn't be missed.

5. Ouro Preto, Brazil. This perfectly preserved 18th-century town is one of the world's greatest enclaves of Baroque architecture. Like a stage set of decorative wrought-iron balconies, pastel-colored mansions, and steep cobblestone streets, this old mining town is home to 13 Baroque churches, including the lavish Nossa Senhora de Pilar.

6. Old Sana'a, Yemen. Situated in a high mountain valley, Yemen's capital Sana'a has been inhabited for more than 2,500 years. Lined with ornate multiple-story mud brick houses with intricate gingerbread facades, the narrow streets of the ancient *medina* quarter seem straight out of the *Arabian Nights*.

7. The Pera Palas, Istanbul, Turkey. Built in 1892 to accommodate guests arriving on the *Orient Express*, the hotel has a faded glamour, and a guest book that lists everyone from Mata Hari to Agatha Christie, who wrote *Murder on the Orient Express* in Room 411. Come for tea and savor Old Stamboul.

A common sight in northern Indiana's Amish Country

ELKHART COUNTY CONVENTION & VISITORS BUREAU

PLACE: .... DATE: ....

"The true mystery of the world is the visible, not the invisible."
—OSCAR WILDE

PLACE: .... DATE: ....

PLACE: .... DATE: ....

PLACE: .... DATE: ....

PLACE: .... DATE: ....

"He who returns from a journey is not the same as he who left."
—CHINESE PROVERB

PLACE: .... DATE: ....

PLACE: .... DATE: ....

PLACE: .... DATE: ....

PLACE: .... DATE: ....

PLACE: .... DATE: ....

"Do not go where the path may lead, go instead where there is no path and leave a trail." —RALPH WALDO EMERSON

PLACE: .... DATE: ....

PLACE: .... DATE: ....

PLACE: .... DATE: ....

"One cannot divine nor forecast the conditions that will make happiness; one only stumbles upon them by chance, in a lucky hour, at the world's end somewhere." —WILLA CATHER

PLACE: .... DATE: ....

PLACE: .... DATE: ....

EIGHT TRIPS
WHERE THE JOURNEY
IS THE DESTINATION

A springtime regatta in the Grenadines

1. Sailing the Grenadines, Lesser Antilles. Whether you charter a yacht with a crew or go "bare boating" and do it yourself, you'll find the Caribbean's Grenadines are a sailor's paradise: 32 islands (some uninhabited and accessible only by boat) strung out like a necklace across 40 miles of water, between St. Vincent and Grenada.

2. Horseback safari in the Masai Mara, Kenya. When the rainy season ends in May, the migrating zebra, antelope, gazelle, and wildebeest begin their search for greener pastures. One of the best ways to see them is on horseback—you'll feel like part of the herd and also visit the *manyattas* (villages) of the nomadic and hospitable Masai people.

3. Pedicab ride, New York City. After enjoying a Broadway show, flag down a pedicab—a bicycle rickshaw powered by an incredibly fit and cheerful young driver—and revel in the sights and sounds of Times Square that whirl around you.

4. Coaching in Bavaria, Germany. Climb into an authentic 19th-century horse-drawn carriage and meander along old coach roads that are practically traffic-free. You'll pass unspoiled meadows, crystal-blue lakes, and rural villages, ending up at Ludwig II's Neuschwanstein Castle, which inspired the palace in Disney's *Sleeping Beauty.*

5. Mount Washington Cog Railroad, North Conway, New Hampshire. The highest mountain in the Northeast, Mount Washington may best be approached by its cog railway. The original "little engine that could" chugs three and a half miles to the mountain's peak, as it's done since 1869, affording dramatic views all along the way.

6. Barging and ballooning, Burgundy, France. Whether you choose to go by water, drifting along the ancient network of rivers and canals, or by air, floating high above the forest-ringed châteaux, barging and ballooning are both serene ways to savor one of France's most beautiful regions.

7. Cycling the San Juan Islands, Washington. In the pastoral San Juans, where cows seem to outnumber cars, you can bike your way back in time to the turn-of-the-century days of farmers and fishermen—or just to the sixties, when handicrafts and pottery were the coin of the realm and to some degree still are.

8. Trekking around Mount Kailas, Tibet. Pilgrims—and trekking tourists—come from all over the world to perform a *kora*, a 32-mile walk around the circumference of this most sacred of Asian mountains to pay homage to the deities. One circuit is said to erase the sins of a lifetime; 108 assures Nirvana.

PLACE: .... DATE: ....

"All journeys have secret destinations of which the traveler is
unaware." —MARTIN BUBER

PLACE: .... DATE: ....

PLACE: .... DATE: ....

PLACE: .... DATE: ....

PLACE: .... DATE: ....

PLACE: .... DATE: ....

"Sail away from the safe harbor. Catch the trade winds in your sails. Explore. Dream. Discover." —MARK TWAIN

PLACE: .... DATE: ....

PLACE: .... DATE: ....

PLACE: .... DATE: ....

"I write entirely to find out what I'm thinking, what I'm looking at, what I see, and what it means." —JOAN DIDION

PLACE: .... DATE: ....

PLACE: .... DATE: ....

PLACE: .... DATE: ....

PLACE: .... DATE: ....

"When a traveler returneth home, let him not leave the countries
where he hath traveled altogether behind him."
—FRANCIS BACON

PLACE: .... DATE: ....

PLACE: .... DATE: ....

EIGHT WAYS TO TRAVEL ABROAD WITHOUT LEAVING HOME

1. Korea Town, West 32nd Street, New York City. New York's Korea Town is only one block long, but if you step inside any one of literally dozens of Korean barbeque restaurants, you'll feel as if you're in Seoul. The lunch crowd is buttoned-down manager types; at night, trendy twenty-somethings fill the air with laughter and the sound of a million cell phone tones.

2. Little Denmark, Solvang, California. Apart from the balmy weather, Solvang is very much like a Danish village, with its old country architecture, windmills, and cobblestone side streets. At Danish Days every September, the locals set up giant pans and cook Aebleskivers—an apple rolled up in a waffle, looking much like a tennis ball.

3. Little Havana, Miami, Florida. Cuba has long been off-limits, so Miami's Little Havana—with its vibrant tropical architecture, home-style cooking, and red-hot nightlife that's all music, madness, and *mojitos*—is the closest most of us will get to the real thing.

4. Fredericksburg, Texas. Settled by German farmers 150 years ago, Fredericksburg is an oddball combination of Marlboro Country and Bavaria—with the latter winning out. You can't take three steps down Main Street without being lured into a beer hall booming oompah music. Even the town's Web site greets you with a hearty "Wilkommen!"

5. Boyle Heights, Los Angeles, California. Once inhabited by Jewish immigrants, Boyle Heights is now the heart of the *barrio*, famous for its Mexican food and colorful murals. In Mariachi Plaza musicians in ruffled shirts and embroidered bolero jackets take up their guitars and entertain the passersby every afternoon and evening.

6. Chinatown, San Francisco, California. San Francisco's Chinatown is inarguably non-Western—especially during the New Year, when fireworks drown out the clack of mah-jongg tiles and a phantasmagorical parade winds past the gilded storefronts, herb and tea shops, and dim sum joints that line its narrow streets.

JOHN ELK III/LONELY PLANET IMAGES

A decorative street in San Francisco's Chinatown.

7. Brighton Beach, Brooklyn, New York. Once nicknamed "the retired poor man's Miami," this neighborhood next door to Coney Island is now known as Little Odessa—home to some 150,000 Soviet immigrants who still favor their cabbage pies, lard sandwiches, strong vodka, and sentimental music.

8. Lafayette, Louisiana. *Laissez les bon temps rouler* is the unofficial motto of the Festival International de Louisiane. Every April there is food, music, and dancing from throughout the French-speaking world, all stirred together in a harmonious—and spicy—gumbo in this distinctly Cajun enclave.

PLACE: .... DATE: ....

PLACE: .... DATE: ....

"Travel is fatal to prejudice." —MARK TWAIN

PLACE: .... DATE: ....

PLACE: .... DATE: ....

PLACE: .... DATE: ....

" J *ourneys, like artists, are born and not made. A thousand differing*
circumstances contribute to them, few of them willed or determined
by the will. " —LAWRENCE DURRELL

PLACE: .... DATE: ....

PLACE: .... DATE: ....

PLACE: .... DATE: ....

PLACE: .... DATE: ....

PLACE: .... DATE: ....

"They change their climate, not their soul, who rush across the sea."
—HORACE

PLACE: .... DATE: ....

PLACE: .... DATE: ....

PLACE: .... DATE: ....

"Every one of us has in him a continent of undiscovered character."
—CHARLES L. WALLIS

PLACE: .... DATE: ....

PLACE: .... DATE: ....

Eight Places to Find the Most Beautiful Females in the World

1. Liberty Island, New York Harbor.
Even with a 35′ waist, 4.6′ long nose, and a greenish cast to her complexion, the Statue of Liberty, or Lady Liberty, is still considered the most beautiful woman in America, if not the world, because of what she represents. Besides, she's French.

Lady Liberty stands tall.

2. Louvre, Paris, France.
If the Louvre held a beauty contest, it would probably be a toss-up between the *Mona Lisa*, Leonardo's enigmatic masterpiece, and the *Venus de Milo*, armless but incandescent.

3. Ipanema Beach, Rio de Janeiro, Brazil. We all know about the "Girl from Ipanema"—it really ought to be girls. A strip of sand, scarcely wider than the thongs worn by its uninhibited sunbathers, it has become the most famous beach in Rio, if not the world—a shrine to sensuality, flirtation, and jaw-dropping beauty.

4. The 16e Arrondissement, Fashion Week, Paris, France. Even the plainest Frenchwoman can seem effortlessly chic, but when the couture houses are showing their collections, the neighborhood swarms with exotic creatures—from slinky super-models and fabulous fashion editors to the kind of women who know you can never be too rich, too thin, or too well dressed.

5. Southhampton, England. *Queen Mary 2*, the younger—but bigger—sister to the famous *Queen Elizabeth 2*, is totally state of the art and of the moment—with a Canyon Ranch Spa and a planetarium on board—but there are plenty of reminders of the golden age of steamships, including wooden deck chairs with thick blankets and a horn you can hear up to 10 miles away.

6. Red Light District, Amsterdam, Netherlands. Registered, regulated, taxed, and represented by a union since 1984, Amsterdam's ladies of the night are as much a tourist attraction as the city's famous Rembrandt Museum. In quaint neighborhood buildings, they sit in large rose-lit windows, reading Dostoyevsky and doing their nails while showing off their wares.

7. Royal Ascot Races, Berkshire, England. Held every June, the Royal Ascot is a chance to ogle the royals as well as the horses, and everyone dresses to the nines, the ladies in fabulous hats and swirling pastel dresses that show off their dewy English complexions.

8. Mount Everest, Nepal. You don't need to climb the world's tallest mountain to experience her majesty. Journey through the lovely Khumbu Valley for breathtaking views of Chomolungma "Mother Goddess of the Universe," as Everest is known to those who live in its shadow.

PLACE: .... DATE: ....

PLACE: .... DATE: ....

"*The noisier the streets, the calmer I become.*" —JOHANN WOLFGANG VON GOETHE

PLACE: .... DATE: ....

PLACE: .... DATE: ....

PLACE: .... DATE: ....

"One doesn't discover new lands without consenting to lose sight of the shore for a very long time." —ANDRÉ GIDE

PLACE: .... DATE: ....

PLACE: .... DATE: ....

PLACE: .... DATE: ....

PLACE: .... DATE: ....

"No journey is too great if you find what you seek." —ANONYMOUS

PLACE: .... DATE: ....

PLACE: .... DATE: ....

PLACE: .... DATE: ....

PLACE: .... DATE: ....

_____

_____

_____

_____

_____

_____

_____

_____

_____

_____

_____

_____

_____

_____

_____

_____

_____

_____

_____

_____

_____

_____

_____

_____

_____

"*Certainly, travel is more than the seeing of sights; it is a change that goes on, deep and permanent, in the ideas of living.*"
—MIRIAM BEARD

PLACE: .... DATE: ....

PLACE: .... DATE: ....

Seven Tasty Reasons to Overindulge

1. Deep-fried Mars bars at A Salt & Battery, New York City. Believed to have originated at a fish-and-chips shop in northeast Scotland, deep-fried Mars bars are available stateside at the oh-so-British chips shop A Salt & Battery. Crispy on the outside, delectably oozy on the inside, talk about double your pleasure! And don't forget to try another Scottish fave, the deep-fried ice cream.

2. Beignets at Café du Monde, New Orleans. You could think of them as French doughnuts because in spite of their tony name, beignets are hunks of dough, fried in cottonseed oil and covered with powdered sugar. Hot out of the fryer, they're delicious, best taken with a strong cup of chicory café au lait.

3. Superdawg classic at Superdawg, Chicago. Superdawg takes a standard Chicago pure-beef hotdog (the kind with skin that bites back), nestles it in a poppy seed bun, and tops it with kosher pickle, golden mustard,

Superdawg mascots Maurie and Flaurie

and Spanish onion, definitely hold the ketchup. Then they add hot peppers, pickled green tomato, and a special atomic green relish. Mmmm!

4. Chicken fried steak at Babe's, Roanoke, Texas. Smothered in creamy white gravy, served with mashed potatoes, creamed corn, and buttermilk biscuits with honey and butter, chicken fried steak is a Texas staple that takes carbo-loading to new extremes. And at Babe's, a north Texas landmark housed inside an old hardware store, you have only two choices: chicken fried steak or fried chicken.

5. Barbecued spaghetti at Interstate Bar-B-Que, Memphis, Tennessee. Poor Elvis. This dish may have been the final nail in his coffin, but don't let that discourage you from tucking into one of Dixie's tastiest, albeit oddest, combos—spaghetti with pork and barbecue sauce served up by one of Memphis's most respected BBQ joints.

6. A Galley Boy and a Cherry Phosphate at Swenson's Drive-in, Akron, Ohio. Dig into the classic American meal at this 1950's-style drive-in. A Galley Boy is a double cheeseburger with two special sauces; accompany it with french fries, onion rings, or fried mushrooms or zucchini, and finish with a bubbly phosphate or a mint whip. It tastes extra good because it's served to you by a carhop.

7. Fried oyster po' boy at Mother's, New Orleans. A "po' boy," the New Orleans version of a hoagie or sub, is two hunks of crisp New Orleans French bread piled high with everything from corned beef to catfish, fried shrimp to fried sausage. One of the most sublime is the fried oyster po' boy. So order one "dresseda" (with lettuce and tomatoes). Don't forget the Tabasco and Creole mustard. Then wash it all down with an ice-cold Barq's root beer.

PLACE: .... DATE: ....

"As you walk and eat and travel, be where you are, otherwise you will miss most of your life." —BUDDHA

PLACE: .... DATE: ....

PLACE: .... DATE: ....

P<small>LACE</small>: .... D<small>ATE</small>: ....

PLACE: .... DATE: ....

PLACE: .... DATE: ....

"B lessed are the curious for they shall have adventure."
—L. DRACHMAN

PLACE: .... DATE: ....

PLACE: .... DATE: ....

PLACE: .... DATE: ....

"The first step in the journey is to lose your way."
—GALWAY KINNELL

PLACE: .... DATE: ....

PLACE: .... DATE: ....

PLACE: .... DATE: ....

PLACE: .... DATE: ....

"I can see now that my travels as much as the act of writing were ways of escape." —GRAHAM GREENE

PLACE: .... DATE: ....

PLACE: .... DATE: ....

EIGHT ACTIVITIES THAT WILL DEFINITELY RAISE YOUR HEART RATE

1. Bungee jumping, Queenstown, New Zealand. Bungee jumping, which originated eons ago as a coming-of-age ritual on the nearby Vanuatu islands, can make your knees weak thinking about it. Queenstown's high-energy approach to fun will get you pumped —and so far, everyone has lived to tell about it, including an 84-year-old grandpa.

2. Rafting the Zambezi River, Zambia. It's no wonder rafting fanatics call it the "Slambezi." Barreling through the narrow basalt gorges at the foot of Victoria Falls, the mighty Zambezi churns up some hair-raising drops and classic white-water rapids.

3. Dune-hopping in Natal, Brazil. Natal features miles and miles of enormous white dunes. Rent a four-wheel-drive beach buggy—or, better yet, leave the driving to a local *buguiero*, who'll pilot your rig across the shifting sands and through vertiginous turns like an Indy-500 driver.

4. Shark Rodeo at Walker's Cay, Abacos Islands, Bahamas. At this old-time rumrunner's refuge, you can swim among a hundred or more sharks, confident that these magnificent creatures gnawing at their frozen "chumsicle" of fish carcass will be too distracted by their snack to be even remotely interested in you.

5. The Kentucky Derby, Louisville, Kentucky. At Churchill Downs, you can't help but give in to the excitement of the Kentucky Derby. Hearing the crowd roar as the Thoroughbreds thunder down the track, you can easily see why the race is billed as "the greatest two minutes in sports."

Thoroughbreds bursting from the gate at the Kentucky Derby.

6. Skiing the Interconnect, Wasatch Range, Utah. Leave the groomed trails and ski the backcountry in an excursion that connects five ski resorts—Park City, Brighton, Solitude, Alta, and Snowbird. Not for bunnies, it offers astounding views and miles of pristine powder.

7. Running with the bulls, Pamplona, Spain. Sometimes it's hard to know the difference between an endorphin high and a testosterone overdose, particularly during the Festival de San Fermin, when a few hundred sangria-fueled lunatics who've read too much Hemingway rush through the streets, pursued by a stampede of snorting bulls.

8. Paragliding Angel Falls, Puerto Ordaz, Venezuela. Angel Falls is 3,212 feet tall, one and a half times higher than the Empire State Building. Try to catch a thermal draft, and your breath, as you tandem-paraglide off the top of the falls— scared stiff maybe, but safe with the instructor strapped to your back.

PLACE: .... DATE: ....

PLACE: .... DATE: ....

"*Travel is as much a passion as ambition or love.*" —L. E. LANDON

PLACE: .... DATE: ....

PLACE: .... DATE: ....

PLACE: .... DATE: ....

" We take to the breeze; We go as we please." —E. B. WHITE,
CHARLOTTE'S WEB

PLACE: .... DATE: ....

PLACE: .... DATE: ....

PLACE: .... DATE: ....

PLACE: .... DATE: ....

"The real treasure, that which we all seek, is never very far; there is no real need to seek it in a distant place, for it lies buried within our own hearts. And yet, there is this strange and persistent fact, that it is only after a journey in a distant region, in a new land, that the way to that treasure becomes clear." —HEINRICH ZIMMER

PLACE: .... DATE: ....

PLACE: .... DATE: ....

PLACE: .... DATE: ....

66 **I** *sought to see the amazing as normal, and the daily as unique, and*
in that swirling paradox I found the joy of travel." —MARY POXON

PLACE: .... DATE: ....

PLACE: .... DATE: ....

PLACE: .... DATE: ....

SEVEN PLACES THAT AWAKEN YOUR INNER CHILD

1. Kennedy Space Center, Cape Canaveral, Florida. The thunderous sound system at the Galaxy Center makes you feel as if you're standing on the launch pad during a Shuttle takeoff, but the real kicks are at the nearby Astronaut Hall of Fame, where you buckle yourself into the G-force centrifuge that simulates a jet fighter training run, or 3-D 360, that will flip you through barrel roll maneuvers.

2. Abu's Camp, Okavango Delta, Botswana. It's a bit like running away to join the circus—joining this elephant "safari" with six adults and a family of youngsters trailing along, tusk to tail. With you atop, the elephants walk at a stately 5 mph and mask your scent, allowing you to get close and view wildlife, which is unthreatened by these gentle herbivores.

Abu and extended family

3. Montreal's International Fireworks Competition, Canada. Every June and July, some 2 million starry-eyed spectators gather on the shores of the St. Lawrence River to see the world's best fireworks techies light up the skies over Montreal with their biggest, most pyromaniacal creations. You're not in Chinatown anymore, Toto.

4. Cannon Beach Sandcastle Contest, Cannon, Oregon. If the pristine beauty of northern Oregon's dramatic coastline is a testament to the majesty of Mother Nature, then the annual Cannon Beach Sandcastle Contest is a testament to man's irrepressible need to play with her—entries have included a Roman ruin with gladiators and chariots, and an enormous head of Shrek.

5. Central Park moonlight ride, New York City. When they're not protesting for cyclists' rights, the enviro group Time's Up leads bike rides around the city, including the monthly midnight spin around Central Park. Is it safe? Definitely. Is it thrilling? You bet your ten-speed it is.

6. The Bitterroot Ranch, Riverton, Wyoming. The Bitterroot is a far cry from your typical dude ranch. The horses are superb, the terrain is wild, and, if you're up to it, the owners will test your mettle with "the rollercoaster," a heart-racing plunge at full gallop, down a series of limestone hills.

7. The Drielandenpunt Maze, Limburg, The Netherlands. Get lost in the largest and most modern labyrinth in Europe, complete with randomly squirting water walls. Set on a hilltop where The Netherlands, Germany, and Belgium meet, the Drielandenpunt Maze makes navigating Henry VIII's Tudor maze at Hampton Court seem like child's play.

PLACE: .... DATE: ....

"*Like all great travelers, I have seen more than I remember, and I remember more than I have seen.*" —BENJAMIN DISRAELI

PLACE: .... DATE: ....

PLACE: .... DATE: ....

PLACE: .... DATE: ....

PLACE: .... DATE: ....

"I soon realized that no journey carries one far unless, as it extends into the world around us, it goes an equal distance into the world within." —LILLIAN SMITH

PLACE: .... DATE: ....

PLACE: .... DATE: ....

PLACE: .... DATE: ....

PLACE: .... DATE: ....

PLACE: .... DATE: ....

"Our battered suitcases were piled on the sidewalks again;
we had longer ways to go. But no matter, the road is life."
—JACK KEROUAC

PLACE: .... DATE: ....

PLACE: .... DATE: ....

PLACE: .... DATE: ....

"The supreme moments of travel are born of beauty and strangeness
in equal parts; the first panders to the senses, the second to mind."
—ROBERT BRYANT

PLACE: .... DATE: ....

PLACE: .... DATE: ....

EIGHT OVER-THE-TOP CELEBRATIONS YOU'LL NEVER FORGET

1. Naadam Festival, Ulaanbaatar, Mongolia. Ever since the time of Genghis Kahn, Mongolians have clung fiercely to their horse-based culture. At the Naadam Festival in July, herdsmen come for two wild days of raucous socializing and unbridled competition in horse racing, archery, and wrestling. The sight and sound of 600 horses charging over the plains is a heart stopper, as is the celebration that follows.

2. Betrothal Festival, Atlas Mountains, Morocco. Every September, before the nomadic Berbers settle in for the winter, they host a betrothal fair, a kind of Moroccan Sadie Hawkins mixer where the single girls do the choosing. With music, dancing, and lots of jewelry on display, the fair lasts for three days, making it feel like a medley of all the weddings you've ever been to.

3. Oktoberfest, Munich, Germany. It's the ultimate party—sixteen days of eating and drinking heartily, and hanging out with boisterous strangers. It begins with a parade led by horse-drawn beer wagons and ends at the fairgrounds with oompah concerts, gut-churning rides, and, probably, a hangover.

4. Sturgis Motorcycle Rally, Sturgis, South Dakota. Begun in 1938, Sturgis became the kind of bacchanal immortalized in *The Wild Ones*. Today it's almost a family destination, with law and order prevailing. But everyone partakes in the hill climbs and concerts, and prowls the streets, admiring the chromed-out "Hogs."

5. The Gypsy Pilgrimage, Camargue, France. At the end of May, the Camargue—known for its pink flamingos, white horses, black bulls, and colorful cowboys—hosts the Gypsy Pilgrimage. More than 20,000 Gypsies fill the streets of the village of Stes.-Maries-de-la-Mer with the chatter of *gitane* and their passionate music.

6. The White Party, Miami Beach, Florida. Twenty years ago, it was a one-night AIDS fund-raiser. The White Party is now a weeklong celebration known for its spectacular events, celebrity watching, and 15,000 gay men and women, mostly young, mostly fit, mostly fabulous—and all breathtakingly gorgeous in white.

7. Opening Night at La Scala, Milan. Opening night (December 7) at La Scala has always been a wonderfully theatrical event— in the audience as well as onstage. And now, after its successful $67 million renovation, it's more glorious than ever.

8. Heilala Festival, Tongapatu, Tonga. King Taufa'ahau Tupou IV celebrates his birthday every 4th of July with a weeklong marathon of beauty contests, yacht races, military parades, concerts, and parties. The whole island turns out, and you are invited, too.

A float at the annual Heilala Festival

PLACE: .... DATE: ....

PLACE: .... DATE: ....

"*The Promised Land always lies on the other side of the wilderness.*"
—HAVELOCK ELLIS

PLACE: .... DATE: ....

PLACE: .... DATE: ....

PLACE: .... DATE: ....

"While you are upon the earth, enjoy the good things that are here."
—JOHN SELDEN

PLACE: .... DATE: ....

PLACE: .... DATE: ....

PLACE: .... DATE: ....

PLACE: .... DATE: ....

PLACE: .... DATE: ....

"*Some parts of the world you make a conscious effort to visit and others have to wait until fate delivers you there.*" —TONY HAWKS

PLACE: .... DATE: ....

PLACE: .... DATE: ....

PLACE: .... DATE: ....

"Own only what you can carry with you; know language, know countries, know people. Let your memory be your travel bag."

—ALEKSANDR SOLZHENITSYN

PLACE: .... DATE: ....

PLACE: .... DATE: ....

EIGHT PLACES WHERE ROCK IS THE STAR

1. Petra, Jordan. In the ancient fortress city of Petra, the houses, temples, and tombs were carved into canyon walls. While some parts have been eroded by time and the elements, others have been miraculously preserved. At dawn and dusk, the desert sun turns the walls a gorgeous pink.

2. The Great Pyramids of Giza, Egypt. A miracle of construction, the Pyramids are one of antiquity's most world-recognized icons. But nothing can prepare you for the awe-inspiring experience of seeing them in person. "From the summit of these monuments," Napoleon cried, "forty centuries look upon you."

3. Giants' Causeway, Northern Ireland. Few attractions are as grand, strange, and astonishing as the Giants' Causeway, a honeycomb of more than 40,000 vertical basalt columns, some reaching as high as 40 feet, created by a volcanic eruption some 60 million years ago.

4. Ayers Rock, Australia. Known by its aboriginal name Uluru, or "giant pebble," Ayers Rock dramatically rises 1,142 feet in the air from the featureless plain around it. Five miles in circumference, and as smooth as a human body, it is considered sacred by the Aborigines. If you see it at sunrise or sunset, you'll understand why.

5. The Hope Diamond, Smithsonian Institution, Washington, D.C. The 45.5 carat Hope Diamond is an exquisite steely blue. Said to be stolen from a statue of an Indian goddess, it has passed through the hands of many owners, including King Louis XIV, Pierre Cartier, King George IV, and Harry Winston. Winston donated it to the Smithsonian, where it continues to dazzle.

6. Rock and Roll Hall of Fame, Cleveland, Ohio. This museum brings to life and pays tribute to the music we all love. It contains more than 100,000 iconic artifacts—including Jim Morrison's scout uniform, Janis Joplin's 1965 Porsche, and Jimi Hendrix's scribbled lyrics and Stratocaster guitar.

7. The Grand Canyon, Flagstaff, Arizona. One of the great, enduring symbols of America, the Grand Canyon is what you see in your mind's eye when you think of the Old West. And in person? The canyon's unearthly colors and inhuman scale provide a truly humbling example of what Mother Nature can do if you give her 2 billion years.

8. Easter Island, Chile. The world's most remote inhabited island, Easter Island is famous for its *moai*, more than 600 huge, elongated stone figures that stare eyeless at the distant horizon. They were carved from the island's volcanic tufa, transported for miles, then raised onto stone altars.

The iconic stone figures of Easter Island

T.C. SWARTZ/TCS EXPEDITIONS

PLACE: .... DATE: ....

PLACE: .... DATE: ....

PLACE: .... DATE: ....

PLACE: .... DATE: ....

"We travel, perhaps, with a secret and absurd hope of setting food on the Hesperides, of running our little boat up a creek and landing in the Garden of Eden." —D. H. LAWRENCE

PLACE: .... DATE: ....

PLACE: .... DATE: ....

PLACE: .... DATE: ....

"Writers and travelers are mesmerized alike by knowing of their destinations." —EUDORA WELTY

PLACE: .... DATE: ....

PLACE: .... DATE: ....

PLACE: .... DATE: ....

PLACE: .... DATE: ....

PLACE: .... DATE: ....

"Go where he will, the wise man is at home."
—RALPH WALDO EMERSON

PLACE: .... DATE: ....

Stop dreaming. Get going!

1,000 Places Checklist

GREAT BRITAIN AND IRELAND

- ☐ **CLIVEDEN** Taplow, Berkshire, England
- ☐ **WINDSOR CASTLE** Windsor, Berkshire, England
- ☐ **CHESTER** Cheshire, England
- ☐ **PENZANCE AND LAND'S END** Cornwall, England
- ☐ **ST. IVES** Cornwall, England
- ☐ **HOTEL TRESANTON AND THE SEAFOOD RESTAURANT** St. Mawes and Padstow, Cornwall, England
- ☐ **CHATSWORTH HOUSE** Bakewell, Derbyshire, England
- ☐ **BURGH ISLAND HOTEL** Bigbury-on-Sea, Devon, England
- ☐ **GIDLEIGH PARK** Chagford, Devon, England
- ☐ **ARUNDELL ARMS** Lifton, Devon, England
- ☐ **THE RISING SUN** Lynmouth, Devon, England
- ☐ **ROYAL PAVILION** Brighton, East Sussex, England
- ☐ **GLYNDEBOURNE FESTIVAL** Lewes, East Sussex, England
- ☐ **THE COTSWOLDS** Gloucestershire and Worcestershire, England
- ☐ **CHEWTON GLEN** New Milton, Hampshire, England
- ☐ **WINCHESTER CATHEDRAL** Winchester, Hampshire, England
- ☐ **OSBORNE HOUSE** Isle of Wight, England
- ☐ **CANTERBURY CATHEDRAL** Canterbury, Kent, England
- ☐ **LEEDS CASTLE** Maidstone, Kent, England
- ☐ **SISSINGHURST CASTLE GARDEN** Sissinghurst, Kent, England
- ☐ **THE LAKE DISTRICT** Lancashire and Cumbria, England
- ☐ **LONDON** England
- ☐ **CHELSEA FLOWER SHOW** London, England
- ☐ **THE CONNAUGHT HOTEL** London, England
- ☐ **TEA AT THE RITZ** London, England
- ☐ **HADRIAN'S WALL** Hexham, Northumberland, England
- ☐ **THE NEWARK ANTIQUES AND COLLECTORS SHOW** Newark, Nottinghamshire, England
- ☐ **LE MANOIR AUX QUAT'SAISONS** Great Milton, Oxfordshire, England
- ☐ **OXFORD AND CAMBRIDGE UNIVERSITIES** Oxfordshire and Cambridgeshire, England
- ☐ **BLENHEIM PALACE** Woodstock, Oxfordshire, England
- ☐ **LUDLOW** Shropshire, England
- ☐ **BATH AND STON EASTON PARK** Somerset, England
- ☐ **CATHEDRAL CHURCH OF ST. ANDREW** Wells, Somerset, England
- ☐ **CUNARD'S QM2 AND QE2** Southampton, England
- ☐ **STRATFORD-UPON-AVON** Warwickshire, England
- ☐ **WARWICK CASTLE** Warwick, Warwickshire, England
- ☐ **SALISBURY CATHEDRAL** Salisbury, Wiltshire, England
- ☐ **STOURHEAD** Stourton, Wiltshire, England
- ☐ **STONEHENGE** Wiltshire, England
- ☐ **CASTLE HOWARD** York, Yorkshire, England
- ☐ **YORK MINSTER** York, Yorkshire, England
- ☐ **SCOTTISH GOLF** Scotland
- ☐ **THE CASTLE TRAIL** Grampian Highlands, Scotland

- [ ] **THE HEBRIDES** Scotland
- [ ] **ISLE OF SKYE AND KINLOCH LODGE** The Inner Hebrides, Scotland
- [ ] **SCOTCH WHISKY TRAIL** Highlands, Scotland
- [ ] **HIGHLAND GAMES** Braemar, Highlands, Scotland
- [ ] **SKIBO CASTLE** Dornoch, Highlands, Scotland
- [ ] **LOCH NESS** Highlands, Scotland
- [ ] **INVERLOCHY CASTLE** Fort William, Highlands, Scotland
- [ ] **AIRDS HOTEL** Port Appin, Highlands, Scotland
- [ ] **BALMORAL HOTEL** Edinburgh, Scotland
- [ ] **EDINBURGH CASTLE** Edinburgh, Scotland
- [ ] **THE FESTIVALS OF EDINBURGH** Scotland
- [ ] **HOGMANAY** Edinburgh, Scotland
- [ ] *THE ROYAL SCOTSMAN* Edinburgh, Scotland
- [ ] **THE MACKINTOSH TRAIL** Glasgow, Scotland
- [ ] **ONE DEVONSHIRE GARDENS** Glasgow, Scotland
- [ ] **BALFOUR CASTLE** Shapinsay, Orkney Islands, Scotland
- [ ] **KINNAIRD ESTATE** Dunkeld, Perthshire, Scotland
- [ ] **ALTNAHARRIE INN** Ullapool, Scotland
- [ ] **THE TROSSACHS** Callander, West Highlands, Scotland
- [ ] **CAERNARFON CASTLE** North Wales, Wales
- [ ] **BODNANT GARDEN AND BODYSGALLEN HALL** Conwy and Llandudno, North Wales, Wales
- [ ] **MAES-Y-NEUADD** Harlech, North Wales, Wales
- [ ] **SNOWDONIA NATIONAL PARK** North Wales, Wales
- [ ] **INTERNATIONAL MUSICAL EISTEDDFOD** Llangollen, North Wales, Wales
- [ ] **PORTMEIRION** North Wales, Wales
- [ ] **PLAS BODEGROES** Pwllheli, North Wales, Wales
- [ ] **HAY-ON-WYE FESTIVAL AND LLANGOED HALL** Hay-on-Wye and Llyswen, South Wales, Wales
- [ ] **DYLAN THOMAS'S BOATHOUSE** Laugharne, South Wales, Wales
- [ ] **TINTERN ABBEY** Monmouthshire, South Wales, Wales
- [ ] **ST. DAVID'S CATHEDRAL** St. David's, South Wales, Wales
- [ ] **DROMOLAND CASTLE** Newmarket-on-Fergus, Clare, Ireland
- [ ] **BLARNEY CASTLE AND BUNRATTY CASTLE** Blarney (Cork) and Bunratty (Clare), Ireland
- [ ] **CORK JAZZ FESTIVAL** Cork, Ireland
- [ ] **KINSALE** Cork, Ireland
- [ ] **ASSOLAS COUNTRY HOUSE** Kanturk, Cork, Ireland
- [ ] **LONGUEVILLE HOUSE** Mallow, Cork, Ireland
- [ ] **BALLYMALOE HOUSE** Shanagarry, Cork, Ireland
- [ ] **GLENVEAGH NATIONAL PARK** Donegal, Ireland
- [ ] **BLOOMSDAY** Dublin, Ireland
- [ ] **THE BOOK OF KELLS** Dublin, Ireland
- [ ] **PUBS AND ST. PATRICK'S FESTIVAL** Dublin, Ireland
- [ ] **RESTAURANT PATRICK GUILBAUD** Dublin, Ireland
- [ ] **THE SHELBOURNE** Dublin, Ireland
- [ ] **ARAN ISLANDS** Ireland
- [ ] **CASHEL HOUSE HOTEL** Cashel, Galway, Ireland
- [ ] **CONNEMARA** Galway, Ireland
- [ ] **GALWAY** Ireland
- [ ] **DELPHI LODGE** Leenane, Galway, Ireland
- [ ] **BALLYBUNION GOLF CLUB** Ballybunion, Kerry, Ireland
- [ ] **DINGLE PENINSULA** Kerry, Ireland
- [ ] **THE RING OF KERRY AND THE PARK HOTEL KENMARE** Kenmare, Kerry, Ireland
- [ ] **SHEEN FALLS LODGE** Kenmare, Kerry, Ireland
- [ ] **KILLARNEY NATIONAL PARK** Kerry, Ireland

- ☐ **HORSE COUNTRY AND MOUNT JULIET** Straffan (Kildare) and Thomastown (Kilkenny), Ireland
- ☐ **ADARE MANOR** Adare, Limerick, Ireland
- ☐ **ASHFORD CASTLE** Cong, Mayo, Ireland
- ☐ **WATERFORD CASTLE HOTEL AND GOLF CLUB** Ballinakill, Waterford, Ireland
- ☐ **WEXFORD OPERA FESTIVAL** Wexford, Ireland
- ☐ **TINAKILLY COUNTRY HOUSE** Rathnew, Wicklow, Ireland
- ☐ **GIANT'S CAUSEWAY** Bushmills, Antrim, Northern Ireland
- ☐ **ROYAL PORTRUSH** Portrush, Antrim, Northern Ireland
- ☐ **MOURNE MOUNTAINS** Newcastle, Down, Northern Ireland

WESTERN EUROPE

- ☐ **BREGENZ FESTIVAL** Bregenz, Austria
- ☐ **DÜRNSTEIN AND THE MELK ABBEY** Austria
- ☐ **OLD GRAZ** Austria
- ☐ **GROSSGLOCKNER ROAD** Austria
- ☐ **LECH AND KITZBÜHEL** Austria
- ☐ **SALZBURG FESTIVAL** Salzburg, Austria
- ☐ **VIENNA** Austria
- ☐ **THE OPERA BALL AND HOTEL IMPERIAL** Vienna, Austria
- ☐ **CATHEDRAL OF OUR LADY** Antwerp, Belgium
- ☐ **BRUGES** Belgium
- ☐ **COMME CHEZ SOI** Brussels, Belgium
- ☐ **LA GRAND PLACE** Brussels, Belgium
- ☐ **LÉON DE BRUXELLES** Brussels, Belgium
- ☐ **MARY CHOCOLATIER** Brussels, Belgium
- ☐ **ABBAYE D'ORVAL** Orval, Belgium
- ☐ **BIARRITZ** Aquitaine, France
- ☐ **THE DORDOGNE AND THE CAVE OF LASCAUX** Aquitaine, France
- ☐ **EUGÉNIE-LES-BAINS** Aquitaine, France
- ☐ **ST.-EMILION** Aquitaine, France

- ☐ **MUSÉE D'UNTERLINDEN AND THE WINE ROAD OF ALSACE** Colmar, Alsace, France
- ☐ **CATHÉDRALE NOTRE-DAME DE STRASBOURG** Strasbourg, Alsace, France
- ☐ **BURGUNDY** France
- ☐ **VÉZELAY AND L'ESPÉRANCE** Burgundy, France
- ☐ **CHAMPAGNE AND CHÂTEAU LES CRAYÈRES** Reims, Champagne-Ardennes, France
- ☐ **LES CALANCHES** Ajaccio, Corsica, France
- ☐ **GIVERNY** Haute-Normandie, France
- ☐ **MONT-SAINT-MICHEL** Haute-Normandie, France
- ☐ **NORMANDY'S D-DAY BEACHES** Haute-Normandie, France
- ☐ **PARIS** Île de France, France
- ☐ **HÔTEL DE CRILLON** Paris, Île de France, France
- ☐ **TAILLEVENT** Paris, Île de France, France
- ☐ **CATHÉDRALE NOTRE DAME DE CHARTRES** Île de France, France
- ☐ **CHÂTEAU DE VERSAILLES** Versailles, Île de France, France
- ☐ **TOULOUSE-LAUTREC MUSEUM** Albi, Languedoc-Roussillon, France
- ☐ **THE CAMARGUE AND THE GYPSY PILGRIMAGE** Languedoc-Roussillon, France
- ☐ **THE WALLS OF CARCASSONNE** Languedoc-Roussillon, France
- ☐ **PLACE STANISLAS** Nancy, Lorraine, France
- ☐ **LOURDES** Midi-Pyrénées, France
- ☐ **LOIRE VALLEY AND DOMAINE DES HAUTS DE LOIRE** Pays de la Loire, France
- ☐ **ÎLE DE RÉ** Poitou-Charentes, France
- ☐ **AIX-EN-PROVENCE** Provence-Alpes-Côte d'Azur, France
- ☐ **ANTIBES AND HÔTEL DU CAP EDEN-ROC** Provence-Alpes-Côte d'Azur, France
- ☐ **AMPHITHEATER OF ARLES** Provence-Alpes-Côte d'Azur, France
- ☐ **AVIGNON AND HÔTEL LA MIRANDE** Provence-Alpes-Côte d'Azur, France

☐ **HOTEL CARLTON INTER-CONTINENTAL** Cannes, Provence-Alpes-Côte d'Azur, France

☐ **HOSTELLERIE DE CRILLON LE BRAVE** Crillon le Brave, Provence-Alpes-Côte d'Azur, France

☐ **EZE** Provence-Alpes-Côte d'Azur, France

☐ **LES BAUX-DE-PROVENCE** Provence-Alpes-Côte d'Azur, France

☐ **MOUGINS** Provence-Alpes-Côte d'Azur, France

☐ **VIEUX NICE** Provence-Alpes-Côte d'Azur, France

☐ **LA FONDATION MAEGHT** St.-Paul-de-Vence, Provence-Alpes-Côte d'Azur, France

☐ **ST.-TROPEZ** Provence-Alpes-Côte d'Azur, France

☐ **VENCE** Provence-Alpes-Côte d'Azur, France

☐ **ANNECY AND TALLOIRES** Rhône-Alpes, France

☐ **CHÂTEAU DE BAGNOLS** Beaujolais, Rhône-Alpes, France

☐ **CHAMONIX AND TOUR DU MONT-BLANC** Rhône-Alpes, France

☐ **COURCHEVEL** Rhône-Alpes, France

☐ **VIEUX LYONS** Rhône-Alpes, France

☐ **RESTAURANT PAUL BOCUSE** Lyons, Rhône-Alpes, France

☐ **MEGÈVE** Rhône-Alpes, France

☐ **LA MAISON TROISGROS** Roanne, Rhône-Alpes, France

☐ **PIC** Valence, Rhône-Alpes, France

☐ **GEORGES BLANC** Vonnas, Rhône-Alpes, France

☐ **THE GRAND CASINO** Monte Carlo, Monaco

☐ **HÔTEL DE PARIS** Monte Carlo, Monaco

☐ **BADEN-BADEN AND BRENNER'S PARK HOTEL AND SPA** Baden-Württemberg, Germany

☐ **HOTEL TRAUBE TONBACH** Baiersbronn, Baden-Württemberg, Germany

☐ **THE BODENSEE (LAKE CONSTANCE)** Konstanz, Baden-Württemberg, Germany

☐ **THE ALPINE ROAD AND ZUGSPITZE** Bavaria, Germany

☐ **THE ROMANTIC ROAD** Bavaria, Germany

☐ **BAMBERG** Bavaria, Germany

☐ **RESIDENZ HEINZ WINKLER** Chiemsee, Bavaria, Germany

☐ **COACHING IN BAVARIA AND NEUSCHWANSTEIN CASTLE** Germany

☐ **ALTE PINAKOTHEK** Munich, Bavaria, Germany

☐ **CHRISTKINDLMARKT** Munich, Bavaria, Germany

☐ **DEUTSCHES MUSEUM** Munich, Bavaria, Germany

☐ **OKTOBERFEST** Munich, Bavaria, Germany

☐ **THE PASSION PLAY OF OBERAMMERGAU** Bavaria, Germany

☐ **REGENSBURG** Bavaria, Germany

☐ **BERLIN PHILHARMONIC** Berlin, Brandenburg, Germany

☐ **BRANDENBURG GATE** Berlin, Brandenburg, Germany

☐ **THE MUSEUM SCENE** Berlin, Brandenburg, Germany

☐ **SANS SOUCI** Potsdam, Brandenburg, Germany

☐ **THE ZWINGER** Dresden, Saxony, Germany

☐ **SUMMER MUSIC FESTIVALS** Bayreuth (Franconia) and Schleswig-Holstein, Germany

☐ **THE RHINE VALLEY** Germany

☐ **COLOGNE'S CATHEDRAL QUARTER** Cologne, Rhineland, Germany

☐ **HEIDELBERG'S SCHLOSS** Heidelberg, Rhineland, Germany

☐ **QUEDLINBURG AND HOTEL THEOPHANO** Sachsen-Anhalt, Germany

☐ **HOTEL VIER JAHRESZEITEN** Hamburg, Germany

☐ **LÜBECK** Schleswig-Holstein, Germany

☐ **SYLT** Schleswig-Holstein, Germany

☐ **WEIMAR** Thuringia, Germany

☐ **CRETE** Greece

☐ **MYKONOS AND DELOS** Cyclades, Greece

☐ **SANTORINI** Cyclades, Greece

☐ **PATMOS** Dodecanese, Greece

☐ **RHODES** Dodecanese, Greece

☐ **SYMI** Dodecanese, Greece

☐ **THE ACROPOLIS** Athens, Greece

☐ **NATIONAL ARCHAEOLOGY MUSEUM** Athens, Greece

☐ **DELPHI** Greece

☐ **EPIDAURUS** Peloponnese, Greece

☐ **MONEMVASSIA** Peloponnese, Greece

☐ **MOUNT ATHOS** Northern Greece, Greece

☐ **HYDRA** Saronic Gulf Islands, Greece

☐ **THE MONASTERIES OF THE METÉORA** Thessaly, Greece

☐ **ALBEROBELLO** Apulia, Italy

☐ **CAPRI** Campania, Italy

☐ **NATIONAL ARCHAEOLOGICAL MUSEUM** Naples, Campania, Italy

☐ **SPACCANAPOLI** Naples, Campania, Italy

☐ **POMPEII** Campania, Italy

☐ **THE AMALFI COAST** Campania, Italy

☐ **POSITANO'S HOTELS** Campania, Italy

☐ **RAVELLO** Campania, Italy

☐ **PAESTUM** Campania, Italy

☐ **THE BEST OF SORRENTO** Campania, Italy

☐ **THE QUADRILATERO** Bologna, Emilia-Romagna, Italy

☐ **PIAZZA DEL DUOMO** Parma, Emilia-Romagna, Italy

☐ **RAVENNA** Emilia-Romagna, Italy

☐ **LA POSTA VECCHIA** Località Palo Laziale, Lazio, Italy

☐ **ROME** Lazio, Italy

☐ **THE HOTEL HASSLER** Rome, Lazio, Italy

☐ **SISTINE CHAPEL** Rome, Lazio, Italy

☐ **CINQUETERRE** Liguria, Italy

☐ **PORTOFINO** Liguria, Italy

☐ **BELLAGIO** Lombardy, Italy

☐ **HOTEL VILLA D'ESTE** Cernobbio, Lombardy, Italy

☐ **PALAZZO DUCALE** Mantua, Lombardy, Italy

☐ **THE MILANESE EXPERIENCE** Milan, Lombardy, Italy

☐ **IL DUOMO** Milan, Lombardy, Italy

☐ **THE LAST SUPPER** Milan, Lombardy, Italy

☐ **LA SCALA OPERA HOUSE (TEATRO ALLA SCALA)** Milan, Lombardy, Italy

☐ **ROCCA SCALIGERA** Sirmione, Lombardy, Italy

☐ **BORROMEAN ISLANDS** Lake Maggiore, Lombardy, Italy

☐ **ROSSINI OPERA FESTIVAL** Pesaro, The Marches, Italy

☐ **URBINO** The Marches, Italy

☐ **LA COSTA SMERALDA** Sardinia, Italy

☐ **AEOLIAN ISLANDS** Sicily, Italy

☐ **VALLEY OF TEMPLES** Agrigento, Sicily, Italy

☐ **MOUNT ETNA** Sicily, Italy

☐ **TWO GEMS OF PALERMO** Palermo, Sicily, Italy

☐ **TAORMINA** Sicily, Italy

☐ **CHURCH OF SAN FRANCESCO** Arezzo, Tuscany, Italy

☐ **FLORENCE** Tuscany, Italy

☐ **THE UFFIZI GALLERIES** Florence, Tuscany, Italy

☐ **VILLA SAN MICHELE AND VILLA LA MASSA** Florence, Tuscany, Italy

☐ **LUCCA** Tuscany, Italy

☐ **MONTALCINO** Tuscany, Italy

☐ **PIENZA** Tuscany, Italy

☐ **IL PELLICANO** Porto Ercole, Tuscany, Italy

☐ **CHIANTI AND SAN GIMIGNANO** Tuscany, Italy

☐ **PIAZZA DEL CAMPO AND THE PALIO** Siena, Tuscany, Italy

☐ **BASILICA OF ST. FRANCIS** Assisi, Umbria, Italy

☐ **PALAZZO TERRANOVA** Città di Castello, Umbria, Italy

☐ **GUBBIO** Umbria, Italy

☐ **IL DUOMO** Orvieto, Umbria, Italy

- [ ] **LA PASSEGGIATA** Perugia, Umbria, Italy
- [ ] **SPOLETO FESTIVAL** Spoleto, Umbria, Italy
- [ ] **CROSSING THE MONT BLANC MASSIF** Courmayeur, Valle d'Aosta, Italy
- [ ] **ASOLO** Veneto, Italy
- [ ] **CORTINA D'AMPEZZO** Veneto, Italy
- [ ] **SCROVEGNI CHAPEL** Padua, Veneto, Italy
- [ ] **VENICE** Veneto, Italy
- [ ] **CARNEVALE** Venice, Veneto, Italy
- [ ] **CIPRIANI HOTEL** Venice, Veneto, Italy
- [ ] **VENICE SIMPLON-ORIENT-EXPRESS** Venice, Veneto, Italy
- [ ] **VERONA** Veneto, Italy
- [ ] **TEATRO OLIMPICO** Vicenza, Veneto, Italy
- [ ] **ANNE FRANK HOUSE** Amsterdam, Netherlands
- [ ] **CAFÉ SOCIETY** Amsterdam, Netherlands
- [ ] **CANAL CRUISES AND TULIP TIME** Amsterdam and Lisse, Netherlands
- [ ] **OUDE KERK** Amsterdam, Netherlands
- [ ] **PULITZER HOTEL** Amsterdam, Netherlands
- [ ] **RED-LIGHT DISTRICT** Amsterdam, Netherlands
- [ ] **RIJKSMUSEUM** Amsterdam, Netherlands
- [ ] **VAN GOGH MUSEUM** Amsterdam, Netherlands
- [ ] **KRÖLLER-MÜLLER MUSEUM** Apeldoorn, Netherlands
- [ ] **DELFT** Netherlands
- [ ] **HET MAURITSHUIS** The Hague, Netherlands
- [ ] **NORTH SEA JAZZ FESTIVAL** The Hague, Netherlands
- [ ] **MANOIR INTER SCALDES** Kruiningen, Netherlands
- [ ] **EUROPEAN FINE ART FAIR** Maastricht, Netherlands
- [ ] **POUSADA RAINHA SANTA ISABEL** Estremoz, Alentejo, Portugal
- [ ] **ÉVORA** Alentejo, Portugal
- [ ] **MARVÃO** Alentejo, Portugal
- [ ] **BUSSACO FOREST** Coimbra, Beiras, Portugal
- [ ] **ÓBIDOS** Estremadura, Portugal
- [ ] **MUSEUM CALOUSTE GULBENKIAN** Lisbon, Portugal
- [ ] **SINTRA** Portugal
- [ ] **MADEIRA** Portugal
- [ ] **ARCOS DE LA FRONTERA** Andalusia, Spain
- [ ] **LA MEZQUITA** Córdoba, Andalusia, Spain
- [ ] **THE ALHAMBRA AND PARADOR DE SAN FRANCISCO** Granada, Andalusia, Spain
- [ ] **SEVILLE** Andalusia, Spain
- [ ] **GUGGENHEIM MUSEUM BILBAO** Basque Country, Spain
- [ ] **SAN SEBASTIÁN** Basque Country, Spain
- [ ] **THE CAVES OF ALTAMIRA AND SANTILLANA DEL MAR** Cantabria, Spain
- [ ] **ÁVILA** Castile and León, Spain
- [ ] **LEÓN** Castile and León, Spain
- [ ] **SALAMANCA'S PLAZA MAYOR** Castile and León, Spain
- [ ] **MESÓN DE CÁNDIDO** Segovia, Castile and León, Spain
- [ ] **LA CATEDRAL DE TOLEDO** Toledo, Castile La Mancha, Spain
- [ ] **CATALAN NATIONAL ART MUSEUM** Barcelona, Catalonia, Spain
- [ ] **LA SAGRADA FAMILIA** Barcelona, Catalonia, Spain
- [ ] **MUSEU PICASSO** Barcelona, Catalonia, Spain
- [ ] **CADAQUÉS AND FIGUERES** Catalonia, Spain
- [ ] **THE WAY OF ST. JAMES AND THE CATHEDRAL OF SANTIAGO DE COMPOSTELA** Galicia, Spain
- [ ] **MADRID** Spain
- [ ] **LA RESIDENCIA** Deià, Mallorca, Spain
- [ ] **RESTAURANT BRUDERHOLZ** Basel, Switzerland
- [ ] **GSTAAD** Bernese Oberland, Switzerland
- [ ] **JUNGFRAUJOCH** Bernese Oberland, Switzerland
- [ ] **KANDERSTEG** Bernese Oberland, Switzerland
- [ ] **MÜRREN** Bernese Oberland, Switzerland

☐ **St. Moritz and the Glacier Express** Engadine, Switzerland

☐ **Schlosshotel** Chasteè Tarasp, Engadine, Switzerland

☐ **Davos-Klosters** Graubünden, Switzerland

☐ **Lucerne Festival** Switzerland

☐ **Park Hotel Vitznau** Vitznau, Lucerne, Switzerland

☐ **Rheinhotel Fischerzunft** Schaffhausen, Switzerland

☐ **Lugano's Splendid Villas** Ticino, Switzerland

☐ **Saas-Fee** Valais, Switzerland

☐ **Verbier** Valais, Switzerland

☐ **Zermatt** Valais, Switzerland

☐ **Winter Alpine Balloon Festival** Château d'Oex, Vaud, Switzerland

☐ **Restaurant de l'Hotel de Ville** Crissier, Vaud, Switzerland

☐ **Montreux Jazz Festival** Montreux, Vaud, Switzerland

☐ **Petermann's Kunststuben** Küsnacht, Zurich, Switzerland

☐ **Dolder Grand Hotel and Kronenhalle** Zurich, Switzerland

Eastern Europe

☐ **Carlsbad** Bohemia, Czech Republic

☐ **Cesky Krumlov** Bohemia, Czech Republic

☐ **Castle District** Prague, Bohemia, Czech Republic

☐ **Charles Bridge** Prague, Bohemia, Czech Republic

☐ **Estates Theater** Prague, Bohemia, Czech Republic

☐ **Old Town Square** Prague, Bohemia, Czech Republic

☐ **U Fleku** Prague, Bohemia, Czech Republic

☐ **Castle Hill** Budapest, Hungary

☐ **The Danube Bend** Budapest, Hungary

☐ **Gerbeaud** Budapest, Hungary

☐ **Gundel** Budapest, Hungary

☐ **Hotel Gellért** Budapest, Hungary

☐ **Rynek Glowny** Kraków, Poland

☐ **Wawel Hill** Kraków, Poland

☐ **Chopin's Birthplace** Zelazowa Wola, Poland

☐ **The Painted Monasteries of Moldavia** Moldavia, Romania

☐ **Count Dracula's Castle** Bran, Transylvania, Romania

☐ **The Trans-Siberian Express** Russia

☐ **The Armory Museum and Red Square** Moscow, Russia

☐ **The Bolshoi** Moscow, Russia

☐ **The Moscow Underground** Moscow, Russia

☐ **Tretyakov Gallery** Moscow, Russia

☐ **Waterways of the Czars** Moscow, Russia

☐ **Nobleman's Nest** St. Petersburg, Russia

☐ **The White Nights Festival and the Grand Hotel Europe** St. Petersburg, Russia

☐ **The Hermitage** St. Petersburg, Russia

☐ **Pavlovsk** St. Petersburg, Russia

☐ **Petrodvorets** St. Petersburg, Russia

Scandinavia

☐ **Aeroskobing** Aero, Denmark

☐ **Hotel d'Angleterre and Kommandanten** Copenhagen, Denmark

☐ **Ny Carlsberg Glyptotek** Copenhagen, Denmark

☐ **Restaurant Ida Davidsen** Copenhagen, Denmark

☐ **Tivoli Gardens** Copenhagen, Denmark

☐ **Kronborg Slot** Helsingor, Denmark

☐ **Louisiana Museum of Modern Art** Humlebaek, Denmark

☐ **Egeskov Castle and Steensgaard Herregaardspension** Kvaerndrop and Millinge, Funen, Denmark

☐ **Falsled Kro** Millinge, Funen, Denmark

☐ **Odense** Funen, Denmark

☐ **Roskilde** Denmark

☐ SKAGEN Denmark

☐ HOTEL KÄMP Helsinki, Finland

☐ THE SAVOY Helsinki, Finland

☐ AINOLA Järvenpää, Lake District, Finland

☐ SAVONLINNA OPERA FESTIVAL Lake District, Finland

☐ ICEBREAKER CRUISE Kemi, Lapland, Finland

☐ SANTA'S VILLAGE Rovaniemi, Lapland, Finland

☐ THE RING ROAD Iceland

☐ KVIKNE'S HOTEL Balestrand, Norway

☐ BERGEN AND TROLDHAUGEN Norway

☐ NORWEGIAN COASTAL VOYAGE AND NORTH CAPE Norway

☐ LOFOTEN ISLANDS Norway

☐ MUNCH MUSEUM AND HOTEL CONTINENTAL Oslo, Norway

☐ VIKINGSKIPHUSET Oslo, Norway

☐ GEIRANGERFJORD Øye, Norway

☐ THE NORTHERN LIGHTS Tromsø, Norway

☐ HARDANGERFJORD Utne, Norway

☐ THE NORTH POLE Norway

☐ GÖTA CANAL Götaland, Sweden

☐ VISBY Gotland, Sweden

☐ THE ICE HOTEL Jukkasjärvi, Norrland, Sweden

☐ DROTTNINGHOLM PALACE AND COURT THEATER Lake Mälaren, Svealand, Sweden

☐ GRIPSHOLM CASTLE Mariefred, Svealand, Sweden

☐ ULRIKSDALS WÄRDSHUS Solna, Svealand, Sweden

☐ THE GRAND HÔTEL AND OPERAKÄLLAREN Stockholm, Svealand, Sweden

☐ STOCKHOLM ARCHIPELAGO Svealand, Sweden

☐ VASAMUSEET Stockholm, Svealand, Sweden

☐ MIDSUMMER EVE Tallberg, Svealand, Sweden

NORTHERN AFRICA

☐ THE GREAT PYRAMIDS OF GIZA Cairo, Egypt

☐ ISLAMIC CAIRO Egypt

☐ KHAN EL-KHALILI Cairo, Egypt

☐ MUSEUM OF EGYPTIAN ANTIQUITIES Cairo, Egypt

☐ DIVING IN THE RED SEA Sinai, Egypt

☐ THE SINAI Nuweiba, Egypt

☐ ABU SIMBEL Lake Nasser, Upper Egypt, Egypt

☐ ASWAN AND THE OLD CATARACT HOTEL Upper Egypt, Egypt

☐ A NILE CRUISE Upper Egypt, Egypt

☐ LUXOR AND THE OLD WINTER PALACE Luxor, Upper Egypt, Egypt

☐ SIWA OASIS Siwa, Western Desert, Egypt

☐ ESSAOUIRA Morocco

☐ FES EL BALI AND THE FESTIVAL OF WORLD SACRED MUSIC Fez, Morocco

☐ IMILCHIL BETROTHAL FAIR Imilchil, Middle Atlas Mountains, Morocco

☐ TREKKING THE HIGH ATLAS Morocco

☐ HOTEL LA MAMOUNIA Marrakech, Morocco

☐ PLACE DJEMAA EL-FNA Marrakech, Morocco

☐ YACOUT Marrakech, Morocco

☐ THE GREAT SAHARA Morocco

☐ LA GAZELLE D'OR Taroudant, Morocco

☐ BARDO MUSEUM Tunis, Tunisia

☐ SIDI BOU SAID Tunisia

EASTERN AND SOUTHERN AFRICA

☐ CHOBE NATIONAL PARK Botswana

☐ JACK'S CAMP Kalahari Desert, Botswana

☐ ABU'S CAMP Okavango Delta, Botswana

☐ OKAVANGO DELTA Botswana

☐ GONDER Amhara Region, Ethiopia

☐ LALIBELA Amhara Region, Ethiopia

☐ OL DONYO WUAS Chyulu Hills, Kenya

☐ **PRIVATE WILDLIFE RESERVES** Isiolo, Central Highlands, Kenya

☐ **ISLAND OF LAMU AND THE PEPONI HOTEL** Lamu Town, Lamu, Kenya

☐ **THE MASAI MARA** Kenya

☐ **LITTLE GOVERNOR'S CAMP** Masai Mara, Kenya

☐ **MOUNT KENYA SAFARI CLUB** Nanyuki, Kenya

☐ **PEMBA CHANNEL FISHING CLUB** Shimoni, Kenya

☐ **RAFTING THE MANGOKY RIVER** Madagascar

☐ **HORSEBACK SAFARIS IN NYIKA NATIONAL PARK** Malawi

☐ **TIMBUKTU** Mali

☐ **MAURITIUS**

☐ **ETOSHA NATIONAL PARK** Namibia

☐ **SKELETON COAST** Namibia

☐ **ALDABRA ISLAND** Aldabra Islands, Seychelles

☐ **DESROCHES ISLAND AND LODGE** Amirantes Island, Seychelles

☐ **LA DIGUE ISLAND** Inner Islands, Seychelles

☐ **STE. ANNE MARINE NATIONAL PARK** Mahé, Inner Islands, Seychelles

☐ **ELLERMAN HOUSE AND MOUNT NELSON HOTEL** Cape Town, Western Cape, South Africa

☐ **TABLE MOUNTAIN** Cape Town, Western Cape, South Africa

☐ **PHINDA RESOURCE RESERVE** KwaZulu-Natal, South Africa

☐ **THE DRAKENSBERG MOUNTAINS** Mpumalanga, South Africa

☐ **SABI SAND GAME RESERVE** Mpumalanga, South Africa

☐ **THE CAPE WINELANDS** Paarl, Western Cape, South Africa

☐ **THE PALACE OF THE LOST CITY** Sun City, Northwest Province, South Africa

☐ **ROVOS RAIL AND THE BLUE TRAIN** South Africa

☐ **CONSTANTIA WINE REGION** Western Cape, South Africa

☐ **THE GARDEN ROUTE** Western Cape, South Africa

☐ **HERMANUS** Western Cape, South Africa

☐ **CLIMBING MOUNT KILIMANJARO** Kilimanjaro National Park, Tanzania

☐ **NGORONGORO CRATER** Ngorongoro Conservation Area, Tanzania

☐ **SAND RIVERS** Selous Game Reserve, Tanzania

☐ **STONE TOWN** Zanzibar, Tanzania

☐ **MURCHISON FALLS NATIONAL PARK** Uganda

☐ **TRACKING THE MOUNTAIN GORILLA** Bwindi National Park, Uganda

☐ **TONGABEZI SAFARI LODGE** Livingstone, Victoria Falls, Zambia

☐ **HWANGE NATIONAL PARK** Hwange, Zimbabwe

☐ **MANA POOLS NATIONAL PARK** Zimbabwe

☐ **MATOBO NATIONAL PARK** Matobo Hills, Zimbabwe

☐ **VICTORIA FALLS** Zimbabwe

☐ **VICTORIA FALLS HOTEL AND LIVINGSTONE ISLAND** Victoria Falls, Zimbabwe

THE MIDDLE EAST

☐ **THE AMERICAN COLONY HOTEL** East Jerusalem, Israel

☐ **CHRISTMAS IN BETHLEHEM** Palestinian Territories

☐ **THE DEAD SEA** En-gedi, Israel

☐ **ISRAEL MUSEUM** Jerusalem, Israel

☐ **THE KING DAVID HOTEL** Jerusalem, Israel

☐ **MASADA** Israel

☐ **MUSEUM OF THE DIASPORA** Tel Aviv, Israel

☐ **OLD AKKO** Israel

☐ **THE OLD CITY** Jerusalem, Israel

☐ **VERED HAGALIL** Galilee, Israel

☐ **JERASH** Jordan

☐ **PETRA** Jordan

- ☐ **AL BUSTAN PALACE HOTEL** Muscat, Oman
- ☐ **NIZWA** Oman
- ☐ **OLD FORTS ROUTE** Muscat, Oman
- ☐ **MADA'IN SALEH** Saudi Arabia
- ☐ **OLD JEDDAH** Jeddah, Saudi Arabia
- ☐ **THE COVERED SOUKS OF ALEPPO** Syria
- ☐ **KRAK DES CHEVALIERS** Syria
- ☐ **OMAYYAD MOSQUE** Damascus, Syria
- ☐ **PALMYRA** Syria
- ☐ **AL-AIN** Abu Dhabi, United Arab Emirates (UAE)
- ☐ **BURJ AL ARAB** Dubai, United Arab Emirates (UAE)
- ☐ **THE GOLD SOUK** Dubai, United Arab Emirates (UAE)
- ☐ **OLD SANA'A** Sana'a, Yemen
- ☐ **SHIBAM** Wadi Hadhramawt, Yemen

EAST ASIA

- ☐ **CLASSIC RESTAURANTS OF BEIJING** Beijing Province, China
- ☐ **THE FORBIDDEN CITY** Beijing, Beijing Province, China
- ☐ **THE GREAT WALL** Beijing Province, China
- ☐ **THE *HUTONGS* OF BEIJING** Beijing Province, China
- ☐ **THE LI RIVER** Guilin, Guangxi, China
- ☐ **HOTEL INTERCONTINENTAL** Hong Kong, China
- ☐ **TEA AT THE PENINSULA** Hong Kong, China
- ☐ **VICTORIA HARBOUR AND VICTORIA PEAK** Hong Kong, China
- ☐ **GARDEN OF THE HUMBLE ADMINISTRATOR** Suzhou, Jiangsu, China
- ☐ **SHANGHAI MUSEUM** Shanghai, Shanghai Province, China
- ☐ **THE TERRA-COTTA WARRIORS OF XI'AN** Xi'an, Shaanxi, China
- ☐ **THE THREE GORGES** Sichuan, China
- ☐ **LHASA** Tibet, China
- ☐ **MOUNT KAILAS** Tibet, China
- ☐ **SUNDAY MARKET** Kashgar, Xinjiang, China

- ☐ **XISHUANGBANNA** Yunnan, China
- ☐ **WEST LAKE** Hangzhou, Zhejiang, China
- ☐ **OLD KYOTO** Japan
- ☐ **WALKING THE NAKASENDO, VISITING THE TAWARAYA** Kyoto, Japan
- ☐ **NARA KOEN** Nara, Japan
- ☐ **SAPPORO SNOW FESTIVAL** Sapporo, Japan
- ☐ **CLIMBING MOUNT FUJI AND RESTORING THE SOUL** Shizuoka, Japan
- ☐ **THE PARK HYATT TOKYO** Japan
- ☐ **TSUKIJI FISH MARKET** Tokyo, Japan
- ☐ **CHERRY BLOSSOM VIEWING** Yoshino, Japan
- ☐ **THE GOBI DESERT** Mongolia
- ☐ **HORSEBACK RIDING IN MONGOLIA** Mongolia

SOUTH AND CENTRAL ASIA

- ☐ **PARO FESTIVAL** Paro, Bhutan
- ☐ **CHOMOLHARI TREK AND THE TIGER'S NEST** Paro Valley, Bhutan
- ☐ **PALACE ON WHEELS** New Delhi, Delhi Territory, India
- ☐ **TOP TABLES** New Delhi, Delhi Territory, India
- ☐ **CHAPSLEE** Simla, Himachal Pradesh, India
- ☐ **LADAKH** Leh, Jammu and Kashmir, India
- ☐ **THE BACKWATERS OF KERALA** Cochin, Kerala, India
- ☐ **THE TEMPLES OF KHAJURAHO** Madhya Pradesh, India
- ☐ **THE CAVE TEMPLES OF NORTHERN MAHARASHTRA** Ajanta and Ellora, Maharashtra, India
- ☐ **TAJ MAHAL HOTEL** Bombay (Mumbai), Maharashtra, India
- ☐ **PALACE OF WINDS** Jaipur, Rajasthan, India
- ☐ **JAISALMER** Rajasthan, India
- ☐ **UMAID BHAWAN PALACE** Jodhpur, Rajasthan, India
- ☐ **THE PUSHKAR CAMEL FAIR** Pushkar, Rajasthan, India

☐ **SAMODE HOTELS** Samode, Rajasthan, India

☐ **THE CITY PALACE AND THE LAKE PALACE** Udaipur, Rajasthan, India

☐ **TREKKING IN SIKKIM** Gangtok, Sikkim, India

☐ **THE TAJ MAHAL** Agra, Uttar Pradesh, India

☐ **THE GHATS OF VARANASI** Varanasi, Uttar Pradesh, India

☐ **THE MARBLE PALACE** Calcutta, West Bengal, India

☐ **THE DARJEELING HIGHLANDS** West Bengal, India

☐ **THE ROYAL SQUARE** Isfahan, Iran

☐ **PERSEPOLIS** Iran

☐ **JALJALE HIMAL** Nepal

☐ **DURBAR SQUARE** Kathmandu, Nepal

☐ **BHAKTAPUR** Kathmandu Valley, Nepal

☐ **MOUNT EVEREST** Nepal

☐ **THE KINGDOM OF MUSTANG** Mustang, Nepal

☐ **FISH TAIL LODGE** Pokhara, Nepal

☐ **ROYAL CHITWAN NATIONAL PARK** Nepal

☐ **THE GALLE FACE HOTEL** Colombo, Sri Lanka

☐ **ESALA PERAHERA** Kandy, Sri Lanka

☐ **THE ROMAN RUINS OF EPHESUS** Turkey

☐ **THE COVERED BAZAAR AND CAGALOGLU HAMAM** Istanbul, Turkey

☐ **HAGIA SOPHIA** Istanbul, Turkey

☐ **KARIYE MUSEUM** Istanbul, Turkey

☐ **MOSQUE OF SULEIMAN THE MAGNIFICENT** Istanbul, Turkey

☐ **THE PERA PALAS** Istanbul, Turkey

☐ **TOPKAPI PALACE** Istanbul, Turkey

☐ **THE WHIRLING DERVISHES OF KONYA** Konya, Turkey

☐ **THE BLUE VOYAGE** Bodrum and Marmaris, Lycian Coast, Turkey

☐ **PAMUKKALE** Turkey

☐ **CAPPADOCIA** Ürgüp, Turkey

☐ **TOLKUCHKA BAZAAR** Ashkhabad, Turkmenistan

☐ **OLD BUKHARA** Uzbekistan

☐ **THE REGISTAN AND SHAH-I-ZINDA** Samarkand, Uzbekistan

SOUTHEAST ASIA

☐ **THE SILVER PAGODA** Phnom Penh, Cambodia

☐ **ANGKOR WAT** Siem Reap, Cambodia

☐ **THE HEART OF BALI** Indonesia

☐ **FOUR SEASONS RESORT AT JIMBARAN BAY** Bali, Indonesia

☐ **UBUD AND THE AMANDARI** Bali, Indonesia

☐ **BALIEM VALLEY** Irian Jaya, Indonesia

☐ **BOROBUDUR AND THE AMANJIWO** Java, Indonesia

☐ **YOGYAKARTA** Java, Indonesia

☐ **LOMBOK** Indonesia

☐ **AMANWANA** Moyo, Indonesia

☐ **TORAJALAND** Sulawesi, Indonesia

☐ **WAT PHOU** Champassak, Laos

☐ **LUANG PRABANG** Laos

☐ **SAILING THE MEKONG RIVER** Laos

☐ **SIPIDAN ISLAND** Sabah, Borneo, Malaysia

☐ **HEADHUNTERS' TRAIL** Sarawak, Borneo, Malaysia

☐ **THE DATAI** Langkawi Island, Malaysia

☐ **PANGKOR LAUT RESORT** Perak, Pangkor, Malaysia

☐ **PENANG** Malaysia

☐ **INLE LAKE** Myanmar (Burma)

☐ **THE ROAD TO MANDALAY RIVER CRUISE** Mandalay, Myanmar (Burma)

☐ **SHWEDAGON PAGODA** Yangon (Rangoon), Myanmar (Burma)

☐ **BANAUE RICE TERRACES** Banaue, Luzon, Philippines

☐ **TAAL VOLCANO** Tagaytay, Luzon, Philippines

☐ **AMANPULO** Pamalican Island, Philippines

☐ **THE EASTERN & ORIENTAL EXPRESS** Singapore

☐ **RAFFLES HOTEL** Singapore

☐ **SINGAPORE'S STREET FOOD** Singapore

☐ **AYUTHAYA** Thailand

☐ **ANCIENT THAI MASSAGE** Bangkok, Thailand

☐ **CHATUCHAK WEEKEND MARKET** Bangkok, Thailand

☐ **THE GRAND PALACE** Bangkok, Thailand

☐ **THE ORIENTAL** Bangkok, Thailand

☐ **THE SUKHOTHAI** Bangkok, Thailand

☐ **THE HILL TRIBES OF NORTHERN THAILAND** Chiang Mai, Thailand

☐ **THE FOUR SEASONS RESORT** Chiang Mai, Thailand

☐ **KOH PHI PHI** Thailand

☐ **KOH SAMUI** Thailand

☐ **PHANGNGA BAY** Krabi, Thailand

☐ **MAE HONG SON** Thailand

☐ **PHUKET** Thailand

☐ **DALAT** Vietnam

☐ **HALONG BAY** Vietnam

☐ **CHA CA LA VONG** Hanoi, Vietnam

☐ **THE FRENCH QUARTER OF HANOI** Vietnam

☐ **HANOI'S OLD QUARTER** Vietnam

☐ **PHO HOA** Ho Chi Minh City (Saigon), Vietnam

☐ **THE REX BAR AND THE BEN THANH MARKET** Ho Chi Minh City (Saigon), Vietnam

☐ **HOI AN** Vietnam

☐ **THE MEKONG DELTA** Vietnam

☐ **SAPA** Vietnam

AUSTRALIA AND NEW ZEALAND

☐ **THE BLUE MOUNTAINS AND LILIANFELS** New South Wales, Australia

☐ **THE HUNTER VALLEY WINE REGION** New South Wales, Australia

☐ **SYDNEY OPERA HOUSE AND THE HARBOR** New South Wales, Australia

☐ **ARNHEM LAND** Northern Territory, Australia

☐ **AYERS ROCK AND THE OLGAS** Northern Territory, Australia

☐ **SEVEN SPIRIT BAY** Cobourg Peninsula, Northern Territory, Australia

☐ **KAKADU NATIONAL PARK** Northern Territory, Australia

☐ **THE TIWI ISLANDS: BATHURST AND MELVILLE** Northern Territory, Australia

☐ **CAPE TRIBULATION** Queensland, Australia

☐ **FRASER ISLAND** Queensland, Australia

☐ **THE GREAT BARRIER REEF AND THE CORAL SEA** Queensland, Australia

☐ **HAYMAN ISLAND RESORT** Queensland, Australia

☐ **HERON ISLAND** Queensland, Australia

☐ **LIZARD ISLAND** Queensland, Australia

☐ **BAROSSA VALLEY** South Australia, Australia

☐ **KANGAROO ISLAND** South Australia, Australia

☐ **CRADLE MOUNTAIN NATIONAL PARK AND THE OVERLAND TRACK** Tasmania, Australia

☐ **FREYCINET NATIONAL PARK AND FREYCINET LODGE** Tasmania, Australia

☐ **THE GREAT OCEAN ROAD** Victoria, Australia

☐ **CABLE BEACH** Broome, Western Australia, Australia

☐ **EL QUESTRO STATION** Kimberly, Western Australia, Australia

☐ **MARGARET RIVER** Western Australia, Australia

☐ **THE BAY OF ISLANDS** North Island, New Zealand

☐ **LAKE TAUPO AND HUKA LODGE** North Island, New Zealand

☐ **WHAREKAUHAU COUNTRY ESTATE** Palliser Bay, North Island, New Zealand

☐ **BUBBLING ROTORUA** North Island, New Zealand

☐ **MARLBOROUGH WINE REGION** Blenheim, South Island, New Zealand

☐ **GRASMERE LODGE** Canterbury, South Island, New Zealand

☐ **THE GRAND TRAVERSE** South Island, New Zealand

☐ **MILFORD SOUND AND DOUBTFUL SOUND** South Island, New Zealand

☐ **MOUNT COOK NATIONAL PARK AND THE TASMAN GLACIER** South Island, New Zealand

☐ **THE HOME OF BUNGEE JUMPING AND JET-BOATING** Queenstown, South Island, New Zealand

THE PACIFIC ISLANDS

☐ **AITUTAKI** Cook Islands

☐ **ISLAND DANCE FESTIVAL** Rarotonga, Cook Islands

☐ **BEQA LAGOON** Beqa Island, Fiji

☐ **HORSESHOE BAY BEACH** Matangi Island, Fiji

☐ **MOODY'S NAMENA** Namenalala Island, Fiji

☐ **JEAN-MICHEL COUSTEAU FIJI ISLANDS RESORT** Savusavu, Vanua Levu, Fiji

☐ **TAVEUNI ISLAND** Fiji

☐ **VATULELE ISLAND RESORT** Vatulele Island, Fiji

☐ **THE WAKAYA CLUB** Wakaya, Fiji

☐ **THE YASAWA ISLANDS** Fiji

☐ **THE MARQUESAS ISLANDS** French Polynesia

☐ **BORA BORA** Society Islands, French Polynesia

☐ **HUAHINE** Society Islands, French Polynesia

☐ **MAUPITI** Society Islands, French Polynesia

☐ **MOOREA** Society Islands, French Polynesia

☐ **HEIVA I TAHITI** Papeete, Tahiti, Society Islands, French Polynesia

☐ **TETIAROA VILLAGE** Tetiaroa, Society Islands, French Polynesia

☐ **THE CORAL ATOLLS OF RANGIROA** Tuamotu Islands, French Polynesia

☐ **CHUUK LAGOON'S GHOST FLEET** Chuuk, Micronesia

☐ **PALAU** Micronesia

☐ **YAP, THE DARLING OF MICRONESIA** Micronesia

☐ **THE HIGHLAND SING-SING FESTIVAL** Mount Hagen, Papua New Guinea

☐ **SEPIK RIVER** Papua New Guinea

☐ **AMBUA LODGE** Tari Valley, Papua New Guinea

☐ **HEILALA FESTIVAL** Nuku'alofa, Tongapatu, Tonga

☐ **KAYAKING THE VAVA'U ISLANDS** Tonga

☐ **SAFUA HOTEL** Savai'i, Western Samoa

☐ **VAILIMA, ROBERT LOUIS STEVENSON'S HOME** Apia, Upolu, Western Samoa

THE UNITED STATES OF AMERICA

☐ **MOUNT MCKINLEY AND DENALI NATIONAL PARK** Alaska, U.S.A.

☐ **KENAI PENINSULA** Alaska, U.S.A.

☐ **THE IDITAROD** Anchorage, Alaska, U.S.A.

☐ **THE INSIDE PASSAGE AND GLACIER BAY** Alaska, U.S.A.

☐ **THE BOULDERS RESORT AND GOLDEN DOOR SPA** Carefree, Arizona, U.S.A.

☐ **CANYON DE CHELLY NATIONAL MONUMENT** Chinle, Arizona, U.S.A.

☐ **THE GRAND CANYON** Flagstaff, Arizona, U.S.A.

☐ **LAKE POWELL** Page, Arizona, U.S.A.

☐ **ARIZONA BILTMORE RESORT & SPA** Phoenix, Arizona, U.S.A.

☐ **RED ROCK COUNTRY** Sedona, Arizona, U.S.A.

☐ **CANYON RANCH HEALTH RESORT** Tucson, Arizona, U.S.A.

☐ **DEATH VALLEY NATIONAL PARK** California, U.S.A.

☐ **THE GOLDEN DOOR** Escondido, California, U.S.A.

☐ **THE GETTY CENTER** Los Angeles, California, U.S.A.

☐ **HOLLYWOOD** Los Angeles, California, U.S.A.

☐ **MONTEREY PENINSULA** California, U.S.A.

☐ **THE PACIFIC COAST HIGHWAY** California, U.S.A.

☐ **HOTEL DEL CORONADO** San Diego, California, U.S.A.

☐ **A TOUR ON SAN FRANCISCO'S CABLE CARS** San Francisco, California, U.S.A.

☐ **CHEZ PANISSE** Berkeley, California, U.S.A.

- ☐ **CALIFORNIA'S WINE COUNTRY** California, U.S.A.
- ☐ **YOSEMITE NATIONAL PARK** California, U.S.A.
- ☐ **ASPEN** Colorado, U.S.A.
- ☐ **HOME RANCH** Clark, Colorado, U.S.A.
- ☐ **MESA VERDE NATIONAL PARK** Cortez, Colorado, U.S.A.
- ☐ **THE MILLION DOLLAR HIGHWAY AND THE DURANGO AND SILVERTON** Durango, Colorado, U.S.A.
- ☐ **ROCKY MOUNTAIN NATIONAL PARK** Estes Park, Colorado, U.S.A.
- ☐ **TELLURIDE** Colorado, U.S.A.
- ☐ **VAIL** Colorado, U.S.A.
- ☐ **ESSEX** Connecticut, U.S.A.
- ☐ **THE MARK TWAIN HOUSE** Hartford, Connecticut, U.S.A.
- ☐ **MYSTIC SEAPORT** Mystic, Connecticut, U.S.A.
- ☐ **LITCHFIELD HILLS AND THE MAYFLOWER INN** Connecticut, U.S.A.
- ☐ **WINTERTHUR MUSEUM** Winterthur, Delaware, U.S.A.
- ☐ **AMELIA ISLAND** Florida, U.S.A.
- ☐ **KENNEDY SPACE CENTER** Cape Canaveral, Florida, U.S.A.
- ☐ **SWIMMING WITH MANATEES** Crystal River, Florida, U.S.A.
- ☐ **EVERGLADES NATIONAL PARK** Florida, U.S.A.
- ☐ **KEY WEST** Florida, U.S.A.
- ☐ **LITTLE PALM ISLAND** Little Torch Key, Florida, U.S.A.
- ☐ **THE DELANO** Miami Beach, Florida, U.S.A.
- ☐ **JOE'S STONE CRAB** Miami Beach, Florida, U.S.A.
- ☐ **SOUTH BEACH** Miami Beach, Florida, U.S.A.
- ☐ **VILLA VIZCAYA** Miami, Florida, U.S.A.
- ☐ **WALT DISNEY WORLD RESORT** Orlando, Florida, U.S.A.
- ☐ **THE BREAKERS** Palm Beach, Florida, U.S.A.

- ☐ **SANIBEL AND CAPTIVA ISLANDS** Florida, U.S.A.
- ☐ **ELIZABETH ON 37TH** Savannah, Georgia, U.S.A.
- ☐ **MRS. WILKES'S BOARDING HOUSE** Savannah, Georgia, U.S.A.
- ☐ **SAVANNAH'S HISTORIC DISTRICT** Georgia, U.S.A.
- ☐ **THE GOLDEN ISLANDS** Georgia, U.S.A.
- ☐ **BIG ISLAND** Hawaii, U.S.A.
- ☐ **KAUAI** Hawaii, U.S.A.
- ☐ **LANAI** Hawaii, U.S.A.
- ☐ **MAUI** Hawaii, U.S.A.
- ☐ **OAHU** Hawaii, U.S.A.
- ☐ **LAKE COEUR D'ALENE** Idaho, U.S.A.
- ☐ **HENRY'S FORK LODGE** Island Park, Idaho, U.S.A.
- ☐ **MIDDLE FORK OF THE SALMON RIVER** Stanley, Idaho, U.S.A.
- ☐ **SUN VALLEY RESORT** Sun Valley, Idaho, U.S.A.
- ☐ **ART INSTITUTE OF CHICAGO** Illinois, U.S.A.
- ☐ **ARUN'S** Chicago, Illinois, U.S.A.
- ☐ **CHARLIE TROTTER'S** Chicago, Illinois, U.S.A.
- ☐ **CHICAGO'S BLUES SCENE** Illinois, U.S.A.
- ☐ **FRANK LLOYD WRIGHT TOUR** Chicago, Illinois, U.S.A.
- ☐ **SUPERDAWG** Chicago, Illinois, U.S.A.
- ☐ **THE GREAT AMISH COUNTRY AUCTION** Shipshewana, Indiana, U.S.A.
- ☐ **IOWA STATE FAIR** Des Moines, Iowa, U.S.A.
- ☐ **THE BOURBON TRAIL** Bardstown, Kentucky, U.S.A.
- ☐ **BLUEGRASS COUNTRY** Lexington, Kentucky, U.S.A.
- ☐ **THE KENTUCKY DERBY** Louisville, Kentucky, U.S.A.
- ☐ **THE FRENCH QUARTER** New Orleans, Louisiana, U.S.A.
- ☐ **THE NEW ORLEANS RESTAURANT SCENE** New Orleans, Louisiana, U.S.A.

- ☐ **MARDI GRAS** New Orleans, Louisiana, U.S.A.
- ☐ **NEW ORLEANS JAZZ AND HERITAGE FESTIVAL** New Orleans, Louisiana, U.S.A.
- ☐ **PRESERVATION HALL** New Orleans, Louisiana, U.S.A.
- ☐ **SONIAT HOUSE** New Orleans, Louisiana, U.S.A.
- ☐ **ACADIA NATIONAL PARK** Maine, U.S.A.
- ☐ **MAINE WINDJAMMER ASSOCIATION** Camden, Maine, U.S.A.
- ☐ **THE WHITE BARN INN** Kennebunkport, Maine, U.S.A.
- ☐ **MAINE LOBSTER FESTIVAL** Rockland, Maine, U.S.A.
- ☐ **OBRYCKI'S** Baltimore, Maryland, U.S.A.
- ☐ **CHESAPEAKE BAY** St. Michael's, Maryland, U.S.A.
- ☐ **THE FREEDOM TRAIL** Boston, Massachusetts, U.S.A.
- ☐ **ISABELLA STEWART GARDNER MUSEUM** Boston, Massachusetts, U.S.A.
- ☐ **LEGAL SEA FOODS** Boston, Massachusetts, U.S.A.
- ☐ **BRIMFIELD OUTDOOR ANTIQUES SHOW** Brimfield, Massachusetts, U.S.A.
- ☐ **CAPE COD NATIONAL SEASHORE** Massachusetts, U.S.A.
- ☐ **WOODMAN'S OF ESSEX** Essex, Massachusetts, U.S.A.
- ☐ **TANGLEWOOD MUSIC FESTIVAL** Lenox, Massachusetts, U.S.A.
- ☐ **MARTHA'S VINEYARD** Massachusetts, U.S.A.
- ☐ **NANTUCKET** Massachusetts, U.S.A.
- ☐ **THANKSGIVING AT PLIMOTH PLANTATION** Plymouth, Massachusetts, U.S.A.
- ☐ **MACKINAC ISLAND'S GRAND HOTEL** Michigan, U.S.A.
- ☐ **BOUNDARY WATERS CANOE AREA WILDERNESS** Ely, Minnesota, U.S.A.
- ☐ **THE NATCHEZ TRAIL** Natchez, Mississippi, U.S.A.
- ☐ **ARTHUR BRYANT'S BARBECUE** Kansas City, Missouri, U.S.A.

- ☐ **BIG SKY** Montana, U.S.A.
- ☐ **THE COMPLETE FLY FISHER** Wise River, Montana
- ☐ **GLACIER NATIONAL PARK** Montana, U.S.A.
- ☐ **TRIPLE CREEK RANCH** Darby, Montana, U.S.A.
- ☐ **BELLAGIO** Las Vegas, Nevada, U.S.A.
- ☐ **THE LAS VEGAS STRIP** Nevada, U.S.A.
- ☐ **THE BALSAMS** Dixville Notch, New Hampshire, U.S.A.
- ☐ **THE LAKES REGION** New Hampshire, U.S.A.
- ☐ **MOUNT WASHINGTON** North Conway, New Hampshire, U.S.A.
- ☐ **CAPE MAY** New Jersey, U.S.A.
- ☐ **ALBUQUERQUE'S BALLOON FIESTA** New Mexico, U.S.A.
- ☐ **ROUTE 66** Albuquerque, New Mexico, U.S.A.
- ☐ **CARLSBAD CAVERNS NATIONAL PARK** Carlsbad, New Mexico, U.S.A.
- ☐ **THE CUMBRES & TOLTEC SCENIC RAILROAD** Chama, New Mexico, U.S.A.
- ☐ **ROSWELL** New Mexico, U.S.A.
- ☐ **INN OF THE ANASAZI** Santa Fe, New Mexico, U.S.A.
- ☐ **THE SANTA FE OPERA** Santa Fe, New Mexico, U.S.A.
- ☐ **TEN THOUSAND WAVES** Santa Fe, New Mexico, U.S.A.
- ☐ **THE ADIRONDACKS** New York, U.S.A.
- ☐ **THE CATSKILLS** New York, U.S.A.
- ☐ **COOPERSTOWN** New York, U.S.A.
- ☐ **EAST HAMPTON** New York, U.S.A.
- ☐ **FINGER LAKES** New York, U.S.A.
- ☐ **HUDSON VALLEY** New York, U.S.A.
- ☐ **NEW YORK CITY** New York, U.S.A.
- ☐ **HISTORIC DOWNTOWN NEW YORK** New York, U.S.A.
- ☐ **MUSEUM MILE** New York, New York, USA
- ☐ **SARATOGA SPRINGS** New York, U.S.A.
- ☐ **THE BILTMORE ESTATE** Asheville, North Carolina, U.S.A.

- [ ] **GREAT SMOKY MOUNTAINS NATIONAL PARK** North Carolina, U.S.A.
- [ ] **THE OUTER BANKS** Duck, North Carolina, U.S.A.
- [ ] **ROCK AND ROLL HALL OF FAME AND MUSEUM** Cleveland, Ohio, U.S.A.
- [ ] **CATTLEMEN'S STEAKHOUSE** Oklahoma City, Oklahoma, U.S.A.
- [ ] **THE OREGON COAST** Oregon, U.S.A.
- [ ] **OREGON SHAKESPEARE FESTIVAL** Ashland, Oregon, U.S.A.
- [ ] **THE LEWIS AND CLARK TRAIL** Columbia River Gorge, Oregon, U.S.A.
- [ ] **CRATER LAKE NATIONAL PARK** Oregon, U.S.A.
- [ ] **WILLAMETTE VALLEY** Oregon, U.S.A.
- [ ] **GETTYSBURG NATIONAL MILITARY PARK AND CEMETERY** Gettysburg, Pennsylvania, U.S.A.
- [ ] **PENNSYLVANIA DUTCH COUNTRY** Lancaster County, Pennsylvania, U.S.A.
- [ ] **BARNES FOUNDATION** Philadelphia, Pennsylvania, U.S.A.
- [ ] **PHILADELPHIA FLOWER SHOW** Philadelphia, Pennsylvania, U.S.A.
- [ ] **PHILLY FOOD** Philadelphia, Pennsylvania, U.S.A.
- [ ] **INDEPENDENCE NATIONAL HISTORICAL PARK** Philadelphia, Pennsylvania, U.S.A.
- [ ] **BLOCK ISLAND** Rhode Island, U.S.A.
- [ ] **CLIFF WALK** Newport, Rhode Island, U.S.A.
- [ ] **BEAUFORT AND THE LOW COUNTRY** South Carolina, U.S.A.
- [ ] **THE HEART OF CHARLESTON** South Carolina, U.S.A.
- [ ] **LOW COUNTRY CUISINE** Charleston, South Carolina, U.S.A.
- [ ] **SPOLETO FESTIVAL USA** Charleston, South Carolina, U.S.A.
- [ ] **THE BADLANDS** South Dakota, U.S.A.
- [ ] **THE BLACK HILLS** South Dakota, U.S.A.
- [ ] **STURGIS MOTORCYCLE RALLY** Sturgis, South Dakota, U.S.A.
- [ ] **GRACELAND AND THE ELVIS TRAIL** Memphis, Tennessee, U.S.A.
- [ ] **MEMPHIS'S RIB JOINTS** Memphis, Tennessee, U.S.A.
- [ ] **NASHVILLE'S MUSIC SCENE** Nashville, Tennessee, U.S.A.
- [ ] **BLACKBERRY FARM** Walland, Tennessee, U.S.A.
- [ ] **SOUTH BY SOUTHWEST** Austin, Texas, U.S.A.
- [ ] **THE MANSION ON TURTLE CREEK** Dallas, Texas, U.S.A.
- [ ] **HILL COUNTRY** Fredericksburg, Texas, U.S.A.
- [ ] **THE MENIL COLLECTION** Houston, Texas, U.S.A.
- [ ] **RIVER WALK** San Antonio, Texas, U.S.A.
- [ ] **BRYCE CANYON NATIONAL PARK** Utah, U.S.A.
- [ ] **MOAB AND RED ROCK COUNTRY** Utah, U.S.A.
- [ ] **MONUMENT VALLEY** Utah, U.S.A.
- [ ] **PARK CITY AND THE WASATCH RANGE** Utah, U.S.A.
- [ ] **MORMON TABERNACLE CHOIR** Salt Lake City, Utah, U.S.A.
- [ ] **ZION NATIONAL PARK** Utah, U.S.A.
- [ ] **MANCHESTER VILLAGE** Vermont, U.S.A.
- [ ] **NORTHEAST KINGDOM** Vermont, U.S.A.
- [ ] **SHELBURNE FARMS** Shelburne, Vermont, U.S.A.
- [ ] **STOWE MOUNTAIN RESORT** Stowe, Vermont, U.S.A.
- [ ] **KILLINGTON AND WOODSTOCK** Vermont, U.S.A.
- [ ] **THE HOMESTEAD** Hot Springs, Virginia, U.S.A.
- [ ] **MONTICELLO** Virginia, U.S.A.
- [ ] **SHENANDOAH VALLEY** Virginia, U.S.A.
- [ ] **THE INN AT LITTLE WASHINGTON** Washington, Virginia, U.S.A.
- [ ] **COLONIAL WILLIAMSBURG** Williamsburg, Virginia, U.S.A.

☐ **SAN JUAN ISLANDS** Puget Sound, Washington, U.S.A.

☐ **PIKE PLACE MARKET** Seattle, Washington, U.S.A.

☐ **THE NATIONAL MALL AND ITS MONUMENTS** Washington, D.C., U.S.A.

☐ **THE SMITHSONIAN AND BEYOND** Washington, D.C., U.S.A.

☐ **WEST VIRGINIA'S WHITE-WATER RAFTING** West Virginia, U.S.A.

☐ **THE GREENBRIER** White Sulphur Springs, West Virginia, U.S.A.

☐ **APOSTLE ISLANDS** Bayfield, Wisconsin, U.S.A.

☐ **CANOE BAY** Chetek, Wisconsin, U.S.A.

☐ **THE AMERICAN CLUB** Kohler, Wisconsin, U.S.A.

☐ **CHEYENNE FRONTIER DAYS** Cheyenne, Wyoming, U.S.A.

☐ **GRAND TETON NATIONAL PARK** Wyoming, U.S.A.

☐ **AMANGANI** Jackson, Wyoming, U.S.A.

☐ **JACKSON HOLE** Wyoming, U.S.A.

☐ **BITTERROOT RANCH** Riverton, Wyoming, U.S.A.

☐ **YELLOWSTONE NATIONAL PARK** Wyoming, U.S.A.

CANADA

☐ **BANFF, JASPER, AND YOHO NATIONAL PARKS** Alberta, Canada

☐ **THE CANADIAN ROCKIES BY TRAIN** Alberta, Canada

☐ **THE GULF ISLANDS AND THE HASTINGS HOUSE** British Columbia, Canada

☐ **HELI-SKIING AND HELI-HIKING** British Columbia, Canada

☐ **NIMMO BAY RESORT** British Columbia, Canada

☐ **WHISTLER-BLACKCOMB SKI RESORT** British Columbia, Canada

☐ **SUN YAT-SEN CLASSICAL CHINESE GARDEN** Vancouver, British Columbia, Canada

☐ **TOJO'S AND GRANVILLE ISLAND** Vancouver, British Columbia, Canada

☐ **PACIFIC RIM NATIONAL PARK** Vancouver Island, British Columbia, Canada

☐ **SOOKE HARBOUR HOUSE AND THE AERIE RESORT** Vancouver Island, British Columbia, Canada

☐ **STUBBS ISLAND WHALE WATCHING** Vancouver Island, British Columbia, Canada

☐ **ROYAL BRITISH COLUMBIA MUSEUM AND THE MUSEUM OF ANTHROPOLOGY** Victoria and Vancouver, British Columbia, Canada

☐ **POLAR BEAR SAFARI** Cape Churchill, Manitoba, Canada

☐ **BAY OF FUNDY** New Brunswick, Canada

☐ **GROS MORNE NATIONAL PARK** Newfoundland, Canada

☐ **CAPE BRETON ISLAND AND THE CABOT TRAIL** Nova Scotia, Canada

☐ **NIAGARA FALLS** Ontario, Canada

☐ **WINTERLUDE AND SKATING ON THE RIDEAU CANAL** Ottawa, Ontario, Canada

☐ **ART GALLERY OF ONTARIO** Toronto, Ontario, Canada

☐ **FOUR SEASONS TORONTO** Ontario, Canada

☐ **PRINCE EDWARD ISLAND** Canada

☐ **CHARLEVOIX** Quebec, Canada

☐ **LAKE MASSAWIPPI** Quebec, Canada

☐ **MONTREAL'S SUMMER FESTIVALS** Quebec, Canada

☐ **VIEUX MONTRÉAL** Montréal, Quebec, Canada

☐ **MONT TREMBLANT RESORT** Quebec, Canada

☐ **CARNAVAL IN THE HEART OF NEW FRANCE** Quebec City, Quebec, Canada

MEXICO AND CENTRAL AMERICA

☐ **LAS VENTANAS AL PARAISO** Los Cabos, Baja, Mexico

☐ **WHALE WATCHING IN BAJA** San Ignacio Lagoon, Baja, Mexico

☐ **NA BOLOM** San Cristóbal de las Casas, Chiapas, Mexico

☐ **PALENQUE** Chiapas, Mexico

☐ **COPPER CANYON** Chihuahua, Mexico

☐ **CERVANTES ARTS FESTIVAL** Guanajuato, Mexico

☐ **SAN MIGUEL DE ALLENDE** Guanajuato, Mexico

☐ **ACAPULCO BAY** Guerrero, Mexico

☐ **TAXCO** Guerrero, Mexico

☐ **ZIHUATANEJO** Guerrero, Mexico

☐ **TEOTIHUACÁN AND THE NATIONAL MUSEUM OF ANTHROPOLOGY** Mexico City, Mexico

☐ **MICHOACÁN** Mexico

☐ **MONARCH BUTTERFLY MIGRATION** Michoacán, Mexico

☐ **LAS MAÑANITAS** Cuernavaca, Morelos, Mexico

☐ **OAXACA'S SATURDAY MARKET AND CAMINO REAL** Oaxaca, Mexico

☐ **CHICHÉN ITZÁ** Yucatán, Mexico

☐ **MAROMA** Yucatán, Mexico

☐ **HACIENDA KATANCHEL** Mérida, Yucatán, Mexico

☐ **CABLE CAR OVER ZACATECAS** Zacatecas, Mexico

☐ **EL DÍA DE LOS MUERTOS** Mexico

☐ **BARRIER REEF** Ambergris Caye, Belize

☐ **MOUNTAIN EQUESTRIAN TRAILS** Cayo, San Ignacio, Belize

☐ **CHAN CHICH LODGE** Orangewalk, Belize

☐ **CORCOVADO NATIONAL PARK** Puerto Jimenez, Osa Peninsula, Costa Rica

☐ **MANUEL ANTONIO NATIONAL PARK** Quepos, Puntarenas, Costa Rica

☐ **CHACHAGUA RAIN FOREST HOTEL** La Fortuna, San Carlos, Costa Rica

☐ **ANTIGUA** Guatemala

☐ **LAKE ATITLÁN** Panajachel, Altiplano, Guatemala

☐ **TIKAL** El Petén, Guatemala

☐ **MARKET AT CHICHICASTENANGO** Quiche, Guatemala

☐ **ROATÁN** Bay Islands, Honduras

☐ **PANAMA CANAL** Panama City to Colón, Panama

☐ **ARCHIPELAGO DE SAN BLAS** Panama

SOUTH AMERICA AND ANTARCTICA

☐ **ALVEAR PALACE AND RECOLETA CEMETERY** Buenos Aires, Argentina

☐ **LA CABAÑA LAS LILAS** Buenos Aires, Argentina

☐ **LAS TANGUERÍAS DE BUENOS AIRES** Argentina

☐ **TEATRO COLÓN AND GRAN CAFÉ TORTONI** Buenos Aires, Argentina

☐ **ESTANCIA LA PORTEÑA** San Antonio de Areco, Buenos Aires, Argentina

☐ **ESTANCIA LA BENQUERENCIA** San Miguel del Monte, Buenos Aires, Argentina

☐ **ESTANCIA ACELAÍN** Tandil, Buenos Aires, Argentina

☐ **ESTANCIA LOS ALAMOS** Mendoza, Argentina

☐ **IGUAZÚ FALLS** Puerto Iguazú, Misiones, Argentina

☐ **ESTANCIAS QUEMQUEMTREU AND HUECHAHUE** San Martín de los Andes, Nequen, Argentina

☐ **PERITO MORENO AND GLACIERS NATIONAL PARK** El Calafate, Patagonia, Argentina

☐ **BARILOCHE** Rio Negro, Argentina

☐ **EL TREN A LAS NUBES AND ESTANCIA EL BORDO DE LAS LANZAS** Salta, Argentina

☐ **COPACABANA** Bolivia

☐ **MERCADO DE HECHICERÍA** La Paz, Bolivia

☐ **EXPEDITION UP THE AMAZON** Belém, Amazonia, Brazil

☐ **VER-O-PESO MARKET AND LÁ EM CASA** Belém, Amazonia, Brazil

☐ **THE ARIAÚ JUNGLE TOWER** Manaus, Amazonia, Brazil

☐ **PANTANAL AND THE CAIMAN ECOLOGICAL REFUGE** Mato Grosso do Sul, Brazil

- ☐ **OURO PRETO** Minas Gerais, Brazil
- ☐ **TIRADENTES** Minas Gerais, Brazil
- ☐ **FERNANDO DE NORONHA** Pernambuco, Brazil
- ☐ **SURFING THE SAND DUNES OF NATAL** Rio Grande do Norte, Brazil
- ☐ **BÚZIOS** Rio de Janeiro, Brazil
- ☐ **PARATI** Parati, Rio de Janeiro, Brazil
- ☐ **CARNAVAL!** Rio de Janeiro, Brazil
- ☐ **COPACABANA PALACE HOTEL** Rio de Janeiro, Brazil
- ☐ **NEW YEAR'S EVE AT COPACABANA BEACH** Rio de Janeiro, Brazil
- ☐ **CORCOVADO** Rio de Janeiro, Brazil
- ☐ **IPANEMA BEACH** Rio de Janeiro, Brazil
- ☐ **RODIZIO AND FEIJOADA IN RIO** Rio de Janeiro, Brazil
- ☐ **CIDADE ALTA** Salvador da Bahia, Brazil
- ☐ **THE FESTIVALS OF SALVADOR** Salvador da Bahia, Brazil
- ☐ **HACIENDA LOS LINGUES** San Fernando, Central Valley, Chile
- ☐ **THE WINE ROADS OF CHILE** Central Valley, Chile
- ☐ **EASTER ISLAND** Chile
- ☐ **PORTILLO** Mendoza, Chile
- ☐ **CRUISING THE CHILEAN COAST** Puerto Montt, Patagonia, Chile
- ☐ **TORRES DEL PAINE NATIONAL PARK** Patagonia, Chile
- ☐ **GOLD MUSEUM** Bogotá, Colombia
- ☐ **CARTAGENA DE INDIAS** Colombia
- ☐ **GALÁPAGOS ISLANDS** Ecuador
- ☐ **SACHA LODGE** Napo River, Ecuador
- ☐ **OTAVALO** Ecuador
- ☐ **THE RIOBAMBA EXPRESS** Riobamba, Ecuador
- ☐ **MONASTERIO DE SANTA CATALINA** Arequipa, Peru
- ☐ **CUZCO** Peru
- ☐ **MANU NATIONAL PARK** Peru
- ☐ **THE NAZCA LINES** Nazca, Peru

- ☐ **LAKE TITICACA** Puno, Peru
- ☐ **PERUVIAN AMAZON** Upper Amazon Basin, Peru
- ☐ **MACHU PICCHU** Urubamba Valley, Peru
- ☐ **COLONIA DEL SACRAMENTO** Uruguay
- ☐ **PUNTA DEL ESTE** Uruguay
- ☐ **ANGEL FALLS** Puerto Ordaz, Gran Sabana, Venezuela
- ☐ **ISLAS LOS ROQUES** Los Roques, Venezuela
- ☐ **ANTARCTICA**

THE CARIBBEAN, BAHAMAS, AND BERMUDA

- ☐ **CAP JULUCA AND THE MALLIOUHANA HOTEL** Anguilla, Lesser Antilles (British West Indies)
- ☐ **SHOAL BAY AND GORGEOUS SCILLY CAY** Anguilla, Lesser Antilles (British West Indies)
- ☐ **ANTIGUA SAILING WEEK AND CURTAIN BLUFF** English Harbour and Vicinity, Antigua, Lesser Antilles
- ☐ **ANDROS ISLAND** Bahamas
- ☐ **COMPASS POINT** Love Beach, New Providence Island, Bahamas
- ☐ **THE COMPLEAT ANGLER** Alice Town, Bimini, Bahamas
- ☐ **DOLPHIN DIVE** Little Bahama Banks, Bahamas
- ☐ **PINK SANDS** Harbour Island, Eleuthera Island Group, Bahamas
- ☐ **SHARK RODEO AT WALKER'S CAY** Abacos Islands, Bahamas
- ☐ **SANDY LANE** St. James, Barbados, Lesser Antilles
- ☐ **K-CLUB** Codrington, Barbuda, Lesser Antilles
- ☐ **GOLFING IN BERMUDA** Bermuda (British Overseas Territory)
- ☐ **THE SOUTHSHORE BEACHES** Bermuda (British Overseas Territory)
- ☐ **BONAIRE MARINE PARK** Bonaire, Lesser Antilles (Netherlands Antilles)

- [ ] **GUANA ISLAND** British Virgin Islands, Lesser Antilles (British West Indies)
- [ ] **LITTLE DIX BAY AND THE BATHS** Virgin Gorda, British Virgin Islands, Lesser Antilles (British West Indies)
- [ ] **NECKER ISLAND** British Virgin Islands, Lesser Antilles (British West Indies)
- [ ] **SAILING THE BRITISH VIRGIN ISLANDS** Lesser Antilles (British West Indies)
- [ ] **SANDCASTLE** White Bay, Jost Van Dyke, British Virgin Islands, Lesser Antilles (British West Indies)
- [ ] **BLOODY BAY WALL AND PIRATE'S POINT RESORT** Little Cayman, Cayman Islands (British West Indies)
- [ ] **CUBA'S JAZZ FESTIVAL** Havana, Cuba, Greater Antilles
- [ ] **LA HABANA VIEJA AND THE HOTEL NACIONAL** Havana, Cuba, Greater Antilles
- [ ] **HEMINGWAY'S HANGOUTS** Havana, Cuba, Greater Antilles
- [ ] **MORNE TROIS PITONS NATIONAL PARK** Dominica, Lesser Antilles
- [ ] **CASA DE CAMPO** La Romana, Dominican Republic, Greater Antilles
- [ ] **ST. GEORGE'S HARBOUR AND GRAND ANSE BEACH** St. George's, Grenada, Windward Islands
- [ ] **BEQUIA** Grenadines, Lesser Antilles
- [ ] **THE COTTON HOUSE AND BASIL'S BEACH BAR** Mustique, Grenadines, Lesser Antilles
- [ ] **PETIT ST. VINCENT** Grenadines, Lesser Antilles
- [ ] **SAILING THE GRENADINES** Lesser Antilles
- [ ] **FÊTE DES CUISINIÈRES AND GUADELOUPE'S FINEST RESTAURANTS** Grande-Terre, Guadeloupe, Lesser Antilles (French West Indies)
- [ ] **GUADELOUPE'S OFFSHORE ISLES** Lesser Antilles (French West Indies)
- [ ] **JAMAICA INN** Ocho Rios, Jamaica, Greater Antilles
- [ ] **JAMAICA'S REGGAE FESTIVAL** Jamaica, Greater Antilles
- [ ] **PORK PIT** Montego Bay, Jamaica, Greater Antilles

- [ ] **ROCK HOUSE AND RICK'S** Negril, Jamaica, Greater Antilles
- [ ] **STRAWBERRY HILL** Irish Town, Jamaica, Greater Antilles
- [ ] **HABITATION LAGRANGE** Le Marigot, Martinique, Lesser Antilles (French West Indies)
- [ ] **FOUR SEASONS RESORT** Pinney's Beach, Nevis, Lesser Antilles
- [ ] **THE HORNED DORSET PRIMAVERA** Rincón, Puerto Rico, Greater Antilles (U.S. Commonwealth)
- [ ] **OLD SAN JUAN** Puerto Rico, Greater Antilles (U.S. Commonwealth)
- [ ] **VIEQUES** Puerto Rico, Greater Antilles (U.S. Commonwealth)
- [ ] **SABA** Lesser Antilles (Netherlands Antilles)
- [ ] **EDEN ROCK** St.-Jean's Bay, St. Barthélemy, Lesser Antilles (French West Indies)
- [ ] **GUSTAVIA HARBOUR & MAYA'S** St. Barthélemy, Lesser Antilles (French West Indies)
- [ ] **THE GOLDEN LEMON** Dieppe Bay Town, St. Kitts, Lesser Antilles
- [ ] **RAWLINS PLANTATION** Mount Pleasant, St. Kitts, Lesser Antilles
- [ ] **ANSE CHASTANET** Soufrière, St. Lucia, Lesser Antilles
- [ ] **LA SAMANNA** Baie Longue, St. Martin, Lesser Antilles (French West Indies)
- [ ] **DIVING WITH TOBAGO'S MANTA RAYS** Speyside, Tobago, Lesser Antilles
- [ ] **ASA WRIGHT NATURE CENTER AND LODGE** Arima, Trinidad, Lesser Antilles
- [ ] **CARNIVAL** Port of Spain, Trinidad, Lesser Antilles
- [ ] **BUCK ISLAND** St. Croix, U.S. Virgin Islands, Lesser Antilles (U.S. Territory)
- [ ] **CANEEL BAY** St. John, U.S. Virgin Islands, Lesser Antilles (U.S. Territory)
- [ ] **HARMONY STUDIOS AND THE REEF BAY TRAIL** Cruz Bay, St. John, U.S. Virgin Islands, Lesser Antilles (U.S. Territory)
- [ ] **MAGENS BAY BEACH** St. Thomas, U.S. Virgin Islands, Lesser Antilles (U.S. Territory)

INTERNATIONAL DIALING CODES AND TIME DIFFERENCES

COUNTRY CODE is the national prefix used when dialing TO the country.

INTERNATIONAL DIRECT DIALING CODE is the international prefix needed when dialing FROM the country.

DIFFERENCE IN HOURS is between the country and GMT (Universal Standard Time).

Country	Country Code	IDD Code	Difference in Hours
Afghanistan	93	00	+4 ½
Albania	355	00	+1
Algeria	213	00~	+1
Antigua & Barbuda	1-268*	011	−4
Argentina	54	00	−3
Armenia	374	00	+4
Aruba	297	00	−4
Australia	61	0011	+8 +10
Austria	43	00	+1
Azerbaijan	994	8~10	+1
Bahrain	973	00	+3
Bangladesh	880	00	+6
Barbados	1-246*	011	−4
Belgium	32	00	+1
Belize	501	00	−6
Bermuda	1-441*	011	−4
Bolivia	591	0010	−4
Bosnia & Herzegovina	387	00	+1
Botswana	267	00	+2
Brazil	55	0014	−3
Bulgaria	359	00	+2
Cambodia	855	00	+7
Cameroon	237	00	+1
Canada	1	011	−3 ½ –8
Cayman Islands	1-345*	011	−5
Chile	56	00	−4
China (PRC)	86	00	+8
Colombia	57	009	−5
Congo	242	00	+1
Congo, Dem. Rep. of	243	00	+1
Costa Rica	506	00	−6
Côte d'Ivoire	225	00	0
Croatia	385	00	+1
Cuba	53	119	−5
Cyprus	357	00	+2
Czech Rep.	420	00	+1
Denmark	45	00	+1
Dominican Republic	1-809*	011	−4
Ecuador	593	00	−5
Egypt	20	00	+2
El Salvador	503	00	−6
Estonia	372	00	+2
Ethiopia	251	00	+3
Fiji	679	00	+12
Finland	358	00	+2
F.Y. Rep. of Macedonia	389	00	+1
France	33	00	+1
French Antilles	596	00	−3
French Polynesia	689	00	+10
Georgia	995	8~10	+4
Germany	49	00	+1
Ghana	233	00	0
Gibraltar	350	00	+1
Greece	30	00	+2
Greenland	299	00	−3
Grenada	1-473*	011	−4
Guam	1-671*	011	−10
Guatemala	502	00	−6
Haiti	509	00	−5
Honduras	504	00	−6
Hong Kong	852	001	+8
Hungary	36	00	+1
Iceland	354	00	0
India	91	00	+5 ½
Indonesia	62	001	+7 +8
Iran	98	00	+3 ½
Iraq	964	00	+3
Ireland	353	00	0
Israel	972	00	+2
Italy	39	00	+1
Jamaica	1-876*	011	−5
Japan	81	001	+9
Jordan	962	00	+2
Kazakhstan	7	8~10	+5 +6
Kenya	254	000	+3
Korea (North)	850	00	+9
Korea (South)	82	001	+9
Kuwait	965	00	+3
Laos	856	14	+7
Latvia	371	00	+2
Lebanon	961	00	+2
Liberia	231	00	0
Libya	218	00	+1
Liechtenstein	423	00	+1
Lithuania	370	8~10	+2
Luxembourg	352	00	+1
Madagascar	261	00	+3
Malta	356	00	+1
Martinique	596	00	−4
Mauritius	230	00	+4
Mexico	52	00	−6 –8
Monaco	377	00	+1
Mongolia	976	00	+8
Morocco	212	00~	0
Mozambique	258	00	+2
Myanmar	95	0	+6 ½
Namibia	264	09	+2
Nepal	977	00	+5 ¾
Netherlands	31	00	+1
Netherlands Antilles	599	00	−4
New Zealand	64	00	+12
Nicaragua	505	00	−6
Nigeria	234	009	+1
Norway	47	00	+1
Oman	968	00	+4
Pakistan	92	00	+5
Panama	507	0	−5
Paraguay	595	00	−4
Peru	51	00	−5
Philippines	63	00	+8
Poland	48	0~0	+1
Portugal	351	00	+1
Puerto Rico	1-787*	011	−4
Romania	40	00	+2
Russia	7	8~10	+2 ½ +10
Rwanda	250	00	+2
Saint Kitts and Nevis	1-869*	011	−4
Saudi Arabia	966	00	+3
Senegal	221	00	0
Singapore	65	001	+8
Slovakia	421	00	+1
Slovenia	386	00	+1
Somalia	252	19	+3
South Africa	27	09	+2
Spain	34	00	+1
Sri Lanka	94	00	+5 ½
Sudan		00 249	+2
Sweden	46	00	+1
Switzerland	41	00	+1
Syria	963	00	+2
Taiwan	886	002	+8
Tajikistan	992	8~10	+5
Tanzania	255	000	+3
Thailand	66	001	+7
Trinidad & Tobago	1-868*	011	−4
Tunisia	216	00	+1
Turkey	90	00	+2
Turkmenistan	993	8~10	+5
Uganda	256	000	+3
Ukraine	380	8~10	+2
U.K.	44	00	0
United Arab Emirates	971	00	+4
Uruguay	598	00	−3
U.S.A.	1	011	−5 –11
Uzbekistan	998	8~10	+5 +6
Venezuela	58	00	−4
Vietnam	84	00	+7
Virgin Islands (U.S.A./U.K.)	1-340*/ 1-284*	011	−4
Yemen	967	00	+3
Yugoslavia	381	99	+1
Zambia	260	00	+2
Zimbabwe	263	00	+2

* The country code for all North America Numbering Plan (NANP) countries is 1; followed by the area code.

~Wait for a second tone.

Numbers may change; consult operator for assistance.

CONVERSIONS AND MEASURES

TEMPERATURE

°F	−40	32	41	50	59	68	86	100	104
°C	−40	0	5	10	15	20	30	38	40

To convert temperatures:
°F to °C — subtract 32 then multiply by ⅝
°C to °F — multiply by ⅝ then add 32

U.S. CUSTOMARY TO METRIC

	If you have	*Multiply by*	*To get*
LENGTH	inches	25.4	millimeters
	inches	2.54	centimeters
	feet	0.3	meters
	yards	0.91	meters
	miles	1.6	kilometers
WEIGHT	ounces (avdp.)	28.35	grams
	pounds (avdp.)	453.59	grams
	pounds (avdp.)	0.45	kilograms
	tons	0.91	metric tons
LIQUID	ounces	0.03	liters
	cups	0.24	liters
	pints	0.47	liters
	quarts	0.95	liters
	gallons	3.79	liters

METRIC TO U.S. CUSTOMARY

	If you have	*Multiply by*	*To get*
LENGTH	millimeters	0.04	inches
	centimeters	0.39	inches
	meters	39.37	inches
	meters	1.09	yards
	kilometers	0.62	miles
WEIGHT	grams	0.035	ounces (avdp.)
	grams	0.002	pounds (avdp.)
	kilograms	2.2	pounds (avdp.)
	metric tons	1.1	ton
LIQUID	liters	33.81	ounces
	liters	4.23	cups
	liters	2.11	pints
	liters	1.06	quarts
	liters	0.26	gallons

WOMEN'S CLOTHING

DRESS, COATS, SUITS, SWEATERS

U.S.A.	6	8	10	12	14	16	18
U.K.	8	10	12	14	16	18	20
Cont. Europe	36	38	40	42	44	46	48
Australia	8	10	12	14	16	18	20
Japan	5	7	9	11	13	15	17

SHOES

U.S.A.	6	6.5	7	7.5	8	8.5	9
U.K.	4.5	5	5.5	6	6.5	7	7.5
Cont. Europe	36	37	37	38	38	39	39
France only	36	37	38	38	39	39	40
Australia	6	6.5	7	7.5	8	8.5	9
Japan	23	23.5	24	24.5	25	25.5	26

MEN'S CLOTHING

SUITS, JACKETS, SWEATERS

U.S.A.	35	36	37	38	39	40	41
U.K.	35	36	37	38	39	40	41
Cont. Europe	46	48	50	52	54	56	58
Australia	92	96	100	104	108	112	116
Japan	S			M			L

SHIRTS (COLLAR SIZES)

U.S.A.	15	15.5	16	16.5	17	17.5	18
U.K.	15	15.5	16	16.5	17	17.5	18
Cont. Europe	38	39	40	41	42	43	44
Australia	38	39	40	41	42	43	44
Japan	38	39	40	41	42	43	44

SHOES

U.S.A.	6.5	7.5	8.5	9.5	10.5	11.5	12.5
U.K.	6	7	8	9	10	11	12
Cont. Europe	40	41	42	43	44.5	46	47
Australia	6	7	8	9	10	11	12
Japan	25	26		27.5	28	29	30

Helpful Web Sites

www.state.gov U.S. DEPARTMENT OF STATE: Information about passports, visas, and travel advisories.

www.travel.state.gov BUREAU OF CONSULAR AFFAIRS: Contact information and locations of U.S. embassies and consulates in foreign countries.

www.tsa.gov TRANSPORTATION SECURITY ADMINISTRATION: Traveler and consumer information on travel advisories and security alerts.

www.who.int/en WORLD HEALTH ORGANIZATION: Vaccinations and immunizations for different countries, general health news, and disease outbreak updates.

www.federalreserve.gov BOARD OF GOVERNORS OF FEDERAL RESERVE SYSTEM: Click on "Recent Statistical Releases" for foreign exchange rates that are updated daily.

http://cybercaptive.com CYBERCAFÉ SEARCH ENGINE: A search engine of over 6,000 cybercafés from over 160 countries. Use the site to find the one closest to you.

Useful Phrases

ENGLISH	Yes	No	Please	Thank you	Hello	Good Bye	How much is it?	Where is the bathroom?
Direct Translations								
FRENCH	*Oui*	*Non*	*S'il vous plaît*	*Merci*	*Bonjour*	*Au revoir*	*C'est combien?*	*Où sont les toilettes?*
GERMAN	*Ja*	*Nein*	*Bitte*	*Danke*	*Guten Tag*	*Auf Wiedersehen*	*Was kostet dies?*	*Wo ist die Toilette?*
ITALIAN	*Sì*	*No*	*Per favore*	*Grazie*	*Buongiorno/ Ciao!*	*Arrivederci*	*Quanto costa?*	*Dov'è un gabinetto?*
PORTU-GUESE	*Sim*	*Não*	*Por favor*	*Obrigado/ a*	*Olá*	*Adeus*	*Quanto custa?*	*Onde é banhiero?*
SPANISH	*Sí*	*No*	*Por favor*	*Gracias*	*Hola*	*Adiós*	*Cuánto cuesta esto?*	*Dónde está el baño?*
Phonetic Transcriptions								
ARABIC	naa<u>h</u>m	laa	min fa<u>d</u>lak	shukran	ahlan/ salaam	ma<u>h</u>as salaama	bikam haaza?	ayn al-<u>h</u>ammaamaat?
GREEK	ne	<u>o</u>khee	paraka<u>lo</u>	efkharee<u>sto</u>	<u>kh</u>erete	<u>kh</u>erete/ ya sa	<u>poso kanee af<u>to</u>?	<u>poo eene</u> ee tooa<u>lete</u>s?
JAPANESE	hai	iie	onegai-shimasu	ariga<u>to</u>	konnichiwa	sayonara	ikura desuka?	otearai wa doko ni arimasuka?
MANDARIN	dwee	boodwee	ching	shieshie	nee hao	dsaijian	na duoshaochain?	tsersuo dsai nar?
RUSSIAN	dah	nyet	pa<u>zhal</u>sta	spa<u>see</u>bah	<u>doh</u>bri dyehn	da svee<u>dah</u>nya	<u>skoh</u>lka <u>eh</u>ta <u>stoy</u>it?	gdyeh nahkhohditsah twah<u>lyet</u>?

Design by Paul Hanson

ISBN-13: 978-0-7611-3832-7; ISBN-10: 0-7611-3832-3

Workman books are available at special discount when purchased in bulk for premiums and sales
promotions as well as for fund-raising or educational use. Special editions or book excerpts also can
be created to specification. For details, contact the Special Sales Director at the address below.

Workman Publishing Company, Inc.
708 Broadway
New York, NY 10003-9555

www.workman.com

Printed in Hong Kong

First Printing: May 2005

10 9 8 7 6 5 4